EUROVISION

A FUNNY KIND OF EUPHORIA

Garry Holland

Updated 2017 version

This is a completely independent, non-official book about the Eurovision Song Contest ('Eurovision') and has absolutely no connection with the European Broadcasting Union, which produces the contest so superbly every year. All opinions expressed are purely personal. Any errors of fact are wholly unintentional.

Please note: This edition contains updates made in October 2017.

Original publication date: May 2016.

Contents

Opening: A Sort of Therapy

"When you're tired of Eurovision, you're tired of life."

The words of Dr Samuel Johnson, eighteenth-century man of letters and slight oddball.

At least I'm sure they'd have been his words, had he lived to see the Eurovision Song Contest pop from its cocoon in 1956 as part of the answer to the age-old question: "how can we stop the peoples of Europe knocking seven bells out of each other on a constant basis?"

Yes, the medium of popular song would add a bit of glitz, gloss and glamour to the post-war drive for reconciliation and recovery – glitz that worthy but rather drab initiatives like the European Coal and Steel Community would simply be incapable of delivering.

So it was, then, that pioneers from seven nations headed off to beautiful Lugano in Switzerland to sing songs, appear on telly and then go away again, after defusing just a little of the mistrust that had consigned Europe to centuries of conflict and underpinned its inhabitants' relentless quest to batter one another to oblivion. And even though Eurovision took those initial, tentative steps several years before I was born, it was destined to evolve into something that's coloured my life much more comprehensively than, say, European Union Directives on the curvature of cucumbers or the straightness of bananas.

Let me be absolutely clear. If you're hoping to read in these pages a disdainful dismissal of the sometimes puzzling but always compelling phenomenon called the Eurovision Song Contest, you've come to the wrong book. My stance on the contest – currently watched each year by around two hundred million earthlings and (I'd like to think) also a much-loved spectacle in nearby star systems as the noise-junk we hurl into deep space reaches other cosmic civilisations – can be summed up neatly in just four words. I ABSOLUTELY LOVE IT.

I love the concept. I love the music. I love the performers. I love the presenters. I love the voting. I love the triumphs, the traumas, the travesties and the interval acts. I love awaiting the release of the double CD before the contest and the triple DVD after it. I love the songs about love, peace and understanding, about coming home and going away, about being heroes, about rising like mythical birds, about being the only one, about the 1940s and about loving for both of us. I love the great, the good, the bad and the Swiss. I love what goes right on the night and I love what goes a bit wrong. From ABBA to Zdob şi Zdub, from Frizzle Sizzle to Fud Leclerc, I absolutely love it all.

Non-believers may scoff at me or fear for my well-being – but they'll just have to accept my deep-seated addiction to this funny kind of euphoria. Because I'm firmly of the belief that, if you're unable to savour the contest's very special qualities on some level or other, you're more world-weary than could possibly be healthy for you and you really do need to have a word with yourself. And that word is 'Eurovision'.

*　　*　　*　　*　　*　　*

Dr Johnson compiled a famous dictionary. 'Eurovision' isn't in it. I've checked. But I did find 'eurhythmy', which apparently means 'harmony' – so he was clearly on the right track. And while the genius of Eurovision may not appear as even the faintest blip on the radar of the literary greats, there's always the option of hearing what a genuine, bog-standard, slightly fixated fan has to say on the subject – which is where this book comes in. For me, you see, the Eurovision Song Contest is an undiluted force for good in a dark and dangerous world. Make no mistake – it's the absolute highlight of my year, like Christmas but with warmer weather and without the unwelcome visitors you're not allowed to say 'no' to (apparently).

Rambling through the dense undergrowth of six tangled decades of Eurovision history, this book presents a *smorgasbord* of memories, suggestions and observations, with proceedings punctuated (in suitable Eurovision fashion) by postcards – in this case, transporting you back to a personal finger-buffet of pivotal contests from yesteryear. When ABBA won. When Jemini didn't. When a German lady pretended to be a jukebox. When much-derided Norway finally came good, on the night Sweden entered a song called 'Bra Vibrationer'. That sort of thing. Basically, it's a multi-flavoured selection box drawn from what, on one level, remains a very simple musical event and yet, on another, is an institution crammed with oddities and paradoxes – not least the fact that an essentially European song contest has, in its time, included competing countries from no less than four continents. Hello, Australia! I keenly await a debut entry from the Pacific Republic of Kiribati at some point in the not too distant future.

Four continents – and that's not even counting Quebec-born Céline Dion's intervention in 1988 when she pipped the UK's Scott Fitzgerald by a single point and gave Switzerland their second and, to date, last victory in the contest. And just for the record, it was indeed Switzerland that carried off that first Eurovision crown in Lugano, as Lys Assia successfully regaled viewers and listeners with 'Refrain' and posted a famous win for her country that wouldn't be repeated until they bussed in Céline thirty-two years later under a flag of convenience.

But I (sort of) digress. And while I'm sort of digressing, let me just say I'm sure that, if Eurovision HAD been invented a fair bit earlier and Dr Johnson and others of his time HAD been able to settle down on a Saturday night in May to witness the event, surrounded by diverse Dutch beers, Scandinavian crispbreads, French cheeses, Belgian pâtés, Icelandic-style yogurts and the sausages and salamis of many nations, the Napoleonic wars would never have happened. I'm a hundred percent certain that the only reason Bonaparte would have spent a cold winter in Moscow would have been to get front-row seats for the Russian National Song Selection Final on the off-chance that those grannies with the big bread oven from Eurovision 2012 (who were presumably small girls back then) were on the shortlist.

I suppose this is a companion volume to an earlier effort about my own talent-light, fiasco-heavy attempts to enter songs for the contest for Austria and the UK. 'Big Dreams, Bum Notes: How Music Led Me to Eurovision Oblivion' may not have redefined literature. But it did let me penetrate the hallowed halls of public service broadcasting as I somehow found myself being interviewed by the legendary Ken Bruce on Radio 2 and by the excellent Dan Chisholm and various other DJs across a gaggle of local BBC and community stations. 'Monster!' as Dr Johnson's dictionary would say, if it had been edited by Nigel Kennedy.

The point is, thanks to my many musical reverses down the years, at least I can claim that these pages are brought to you by someone who's genuinely suffered near-mortal damage to their self-esteem for the Eurovision cause – and who still harbours wild dreams of hearing one of his iffy songs grace the contest, where it can be raucously acclaimed by flag-waving, face-painted fans in feather boas from all the great Eurovision nations, and from all the other ones too.

But before we begin, most importantly of all, let me dedicate this book to you, my fellow Eurovision fan. We few, we happy few, we band of brothers and sisters – only we REALLY understand, don't we? Only we really 'get' it. It's hard to be a visionary – and a Eurovision visionary above all. Yes, like you, I've been there. I know what it's like when you tell a non-believer you're a massive Eurovision fan and it's the high point of your year – and then feel the need, thanks to a sort of Pavlov's dog conditioned response, to follow up your confession by blurting out the words "no, really".

It's that look they give you. Even as you utter the words, it's the slight but noticeable widening and then narrowing of the eyes as they realise you're serious and they're faced with a snap decision: whether to keep their response polite or just take the mick. Plus it's the clear assumption – sometimes, but not always, unspoken – that there must be something majorly wrong with you. But do you know what? WE – DON'T – CARE! Our 'Euphoria' is, quite simply, unquenchable and Loreen's steamroller of a winner from 2012 is as good a rallying point as any.

Maybe a love of Eurovision IS a beautiful sickness – a beautiful mess, if you like. Maybe it IS a kind of madness. Or maybe not. But if it is, think of this book as a sort of therapy. For me. For you. For every obsessive and every addict who ever looked at a calendar and took the trouble to calculate, using their own fingers and someone else's if necessary, exactly how many weeks to go until the biggest event of the year. Because, as I hope you agree – or at least will do after ploughing through these pages – what would life be without Eurovision? Huh! It would barely be any life at all. Just imagine how all our lives would be diminished if we'd never witnessed Ilinca and Alex Florea blasting through 'Yodel It!' this year, or seen Francesco Gabbani do 'Occidentali's Karma' via the live link to the 2017 Sanremo Festival. Watching the two of those back to back to back to back to back is as good a 'bad day' antidote as I've ever stumbled upon.

Yes, for all Dr Johnson's plucky efforts, there really is only one word that adequately describes the Eurovision Song Contest and our collective, irreversible, euphoric love for it. As the only viable candidate for Earth President, Conchita, would say: unstoppable!

Postcard: Saturday 6th April 1974

When it comes to dating systems, I'm still entirely old school. For me it's still BC and AD and as for all that Before the Common Era stuff – not so much. But for the purposes of this book I'll shelve personal preferences and recognise that Eurovision history can, should and indeed must be divided into two distinct eras with 1974 acting as Year Zero – the meeting-point between BCE (Before Colossal Eurovision) and what we might term the modern world. For the second of these eras, I'd nevertheless be tempted to stick with AD, as long as it stands for 'ABBA did it'.

Yes, ABBA. Unarguably the contest's premium product, their name and Eurovision are, if not exactly synonymous, certainly fated to be linked for all time in a kind of inextricable game of word association. So for the first of these postcards, let's rewind the clock to that famous victory in Brighton, a town previously best known for having one Georgian seaside palace, two piers and three epic pubs (or so I was once told by someone who'd been there). Yes, Brighton – a town which, if you believed the tourist-luring travelogue that kicked off the contest as soon as Charpentier's Eurovision theme melted away at the top of the show, had once had an Edwardian heyday but was now principally a haven for toby jugs and a mind-numbing abundance of fresh fruit, as well as bluff, salty sea-dogs straight off the set of 'Peter Grimes'.

Entrusted to the safe hands of the BBC and with the imperious Katie Boyle presiding over the evening's proceedings at the Brighton Dome – with Katie imperiously looking and sounding for all the world like a high-class Mrs Thatcher tribute act – here was an event blissfully unaware that the wind of change was about to brush its face, burst its time bubble and give it a long overdue veneer of modernity. Adorned by a pretty basic scoreboard and a live orchestra teeming with shimmering strings and rasping brass under the guidance of the legendary Ronnie Hazlehurst, here was a show whose future claim to be historic can hardly have been guessed at by any of those women sitting in the audience resplendent in their evening gowns, or any of those men in their dinner jackets, bow-ties and general 1970s geeky hirsuteness.

But before the audience get as far as ABBA they've got to enjoy or endure seven other acts, part of an overall field of seventeen runners and riders, though with France absent this time round due to the sad death of President Pompidou. (I don't mean that the late President had been earmarked to sing the French entry, just that his funeral had been scheduled for Eurovision Day.) That's seventeen countries huddled together in the part of Europe not in the grip of the Soviet Bloc, as the contest's Long March eastwards is still two decades away. The most exotic nation on show is therefore non-aligned communist Yugoslavia, who bring a somewhat diluted air of Cold War intrigue to proceedings, much as they did to 'It's a Knockout' (a.k.a. 'Jeux Sans Frontières') for several series and quite a lot of mini-marathons.

First up, it's Finland, with their introductory postcard incongruously accompanied by a pub piano that sounds less Helsinki, more London Borough of Haringey. And the song itself – delivered by piano-bound Carita, who's vaguely reminiscent of the late, great Victoria Wood when she used to do all those self-penned ditties on 'That's Life!' – doesn't make a huge amount of impact as its search for that elusive killer hook ultimately proves pretty fruitless. Unlike Brighton.

Now perhaps the best-known least-known fact about the Eurovision Song Contest is that no country has ever won the thing singing second in the Grand Final. And this time round the graveyard slot has fallen to the host nation – a nation of (judging from the UK's pre-song postcard) beefeaters, bowler hats, top hats and English-born Australian singers. Yes, it's none other than Olivia Newton-

John who's drawn the short straw of trying to bring the big one home for the Brits for the first time since Lulu took twenty-five percent of the spoils in the Madrid fiasco five years ago (recounted in gory detail in Chapter 3).

At the end of the postcard, Olivia coquettishly twirls a pink parasol before we're back in the Brighton Dome and Nick Ingman – looking slightly like a 'Nationwide' reporter about to do a to-camera piece on a skateboarding duck – propels himself to the front of the orchestra to take care of the baton-wielding duties. But to be brutally truthful, despite the best efforts of Olivia and Nick and the rapturous reception it receives from the hairy home crowd, 'Long Live Love' never really breaks free from a kind of quasi-oompah straitjacket.

Spain fare little better, despite the clear potential of their guitar-twirling singer Peret, who seems to have pioneered a unique approach to ensuring audio fidelity by taking to the stage with a big microphone literally bound into and protruding from his necktie. Very odd. The song is as Spanish as it's possible to get and fuels the suspicion that no-one tonight is thinking about venturing anywhere near the edge of their comfort zone, let alone beyond it. Similarly, Norway and Greece (bouzouki and all) do nothing to dispel the notion that this really could be just another feast of fairly middle-of-the-road music where dresses are long, backing singers are strictly static and Glam Rock was just a bad dream that happened somewhere underneath all that hair growing out of the magnificent Roy Wood's magnificent head.

So if Eurovision, steeped in a big dollop of mid-1970s complacency, might perhaps be seen as equivalent to poor old Bill Grundy, where on earth are we going to find our Sex Pistols tonight to shatter the consensus and propel us if not into the future, at least within hailing distance of the present?

But wait! It's song six and we've actually found a band! With long-haired geezers and everything! And an actual guitar riff! And hopefully a hook that I'll be able to recall twenty seconds after the song's finished! Yes, the Israeli entry has arrived and don't let those tank-tops fool you for one moment. Because these boys have got a drum kit and four – count them – yes, FOUR guitars! But any comparisons to Blue Öyster Cult prove slightly premature as the song quickly descends into a fudge of folkiness reminiscent of a November tramp across the expanses of Exmoor's boggiest corners.

Arguably the most pleasing aspect of the Israeli entry has been the band's excellent name: Poogy. But even that's overshadowed by the entry from non-aligned communist Yugoslavia, who've presumably just completed an 'It's a Knockout' mini-marathon throwing wet sponges at Germans spinning on a giant greased turntable while trying to catch rubber fish. But here they are now, resplendent in satin catsuit-type affairs of every conceivable deafening colour and going by the somewhat unfortunate but rather wonderful name of Korni Group. The song starts and ends with the gratuitous bang of a gong but, unless you're fluent in Serbo-Croat, it's impossible to tell what it's actually about. Possibly an ode in praise of better-than-anticipated tractor factory output figures – but that really is just my very ill-informed, very Cold War-coloured guess.

*   *   *   *   *   *

Let's not get ahead of ourselves here. This may be the moment when the world at large gets its first-ever glimpse of ABBA (or 'the ABBA group' as David Vine immortally described them on the BBC TV commentary). But that first glimpse isn't of sparkling Agnetha and glittering Frida charging downstage to belt out a bangin' version of 'Waterloo', flanked by Björn with star guitar and clumpy silver boots and the sainted, bearded Benny planted firmly behind a white grand piano, with someone going "yep!" during the intro. No, our first look at them is the shot of the quartet that graces the preliminary postcard.

And what are we to make of them? Is there any clue that these four people from the icy fastness of Scandinavia are about to shred the rulebook and blatantly ignore the 'keep it worthy but dull' guideline that all the other acts so far seem to have faithfully adhered to? There's Björn beaming in a pink satin jacket, Agnetha radiant with her security pass in full view, Frida in a cracking wide-brimmed hat and presenting more of a cool-and-moody Garbo-esque visage to the world, then the sainted Benny stuck on the end with his beard.

But from the moment Sven-Olof Walldorf appears on the scene and takes command of the orchestra in a cut-price period outfit that, in all honesty, looks less Napoleon Bonaparte and more Mr Midshipman Hornblower, it's evident that something very strange is afoot – and that Sweden might well have entered a completely different contest from the rest of tonight's competing countries. ABBA bring swing, swag and a swashbuckling abandon to the proceedings that's almost jarring when you watch it back now, let alone at the time – though let's not get too revisionist as you'd still be hard-pressed to predict, merely on the basis of this brief intrusion of a proper pop ripple into the docile 1970s Eurovision millpond, that the purveyors of this surgical Glam Rock injection are on the brink of eight years of global mega-success.

And at this point, of course, there's absolutely no guarantee that these rulebook-ripping Swedes are going to win. Will their bold entry prove to be just one more *cul-de-sac* in the Eurovision A to Z of misguided losers who saw their dreams battered and shattered by a bland ballad or a dose of Eurovision biff-bang-bong cobblers? Well, there appears to be very little to fear from Luxembourg, Monaco or Belgium – though the last of these entries provides some food for thought as the singer of 'Fleur de Liberté' ('Flower of

Freedom'), Jacques Hustin, seems to want us to join him on the barricades. Not tonight, Jacques. It's Eurovision.

But then on come Dutch male/female duo Mouth & MacNeal to perform their colourful song 'I See a Star' – with Mouth making a big visual statement by channelling a bold blend of Roy Wood and Lord Salisbury. Replete with puppets of the duo fixed to the top of a mini barrel organ, this may be edging towards 'zany' but it's clearly going to be very competitive. Only the barrel organ and somewhat superfluous bongos militate against the modern feel of a very natural and engaging performance of a very classy, very jolly song. Make no mistake. This could win. Mouth & MacNeal may even be slight favourites in some people's books.

Which is more than you could probably say for Ireland, to be honest. Or for Germany's Cindy and Bert, who appear to be some sort of Mary Hopkin/Peter Purves tribute act, with baton duties performed by the splendidly named Werner Scharfenberger, the sheer length of whose caption at the bottom of the picture demonstrates just why widescreen TV simply had to be invented. Switzerland, Portugal – no thanks. Which just leaves Italy, represented by Eurovision big-hitter Gigliola Cinquetti, winner of the contest way back in 1964 at the age of just sixteen and now keen to repeat the trick a full decade down the line.

As Gigliola acclimatises herself to her three-tier skirt, her song 'Si' ('Yes') starts off disconcertingly like something from the soundtrack of 'The Wicker Man'. And though this ballad, for me anyway, is basically one of those melodious but conservative Italian tunes that conjures up images of package tours to Rimini, it's pretty clear that this is going to pose the most serious competition tonight from the 'traditional' Eurovision camp and give both ABBA and Mouth & MacNeal a real run for their respective pre-Euro currencies.

*   *   *   *   *   *

Overall, taken in the round, across the board and all that stuff, I think it's fair to say that this has been a bit of a low-key evening. And in that spirit, here come The Wombles. Yes, 1974's interval act is film footage of these furry favourites running through a medley of two of their biggest hits, 'The Wombling Song' and the infectious singalong anthem 'Remember You're a Womble' (something that's presumably pretty hard to forget when you're trapped inside a Great Uncle Bulgaria costume). I suppose it's a good job they didn't let them loose in the Brighton Dome to Womble up all the rubbish on the Big Night. They may well have felt duty-bound to walk off with at least a third of the entries, a few of which arguably sounded recycled anyway and so may have needed to be placed in a separate bin.

But now it's crunch time. The voting – that most derided and mistrusted of the multitude of different components of Eurovision's coat of many colours. And as this is 1974, there's barely a whiff of democracy in evidence. Indeed, this seems to be pure oligarchy at work with each country's jury comprising ten members, as the imperious Katie Boyle explains, and not a hint of a public vote in sight. Yes, the musical fate of half a continent lies squarely in the hands of just a hundred and seventy people whose faces we'll never see, whose names we'll never know, whose record collections we can only guess at and who may spend their evenings listening to repeated plays of old *schlager* hits on a clapped-out Dansette record player. To ensure fair play, however – or whatever passes for fair play where an electorate of just a hundred and seventy people are concerned – here comes the official European Broadcasting Union Voting Scrutineer, the legendary Clifford Brown. He's clearly not a man to be trifled with and, I'd say, is thankfully sure to put up with precisely zero lip or nonsense from anyone involved in the painstaking (and indeed mildly painful) ritual that's now about to unfold.

Finland are first to vote down the phone line. They've ten points to dish out and it's five – yes, FIVE – to Sweden! Two to Italy. The leftover scraps of one point each go to the UK, the Netherlands and Yugoslavia. Looks like those tractor factory output figures may have had some effect after all. But ABBA are comfortably in the lead and it's a lead they'll never relinquish as the tortuous process unwinds – despite (and here comes Eurovision's second-best-known least-known fact) the Swedish foursome's receipt of precisely *'nul points'* from the UK jury, which brazenly awards five to Italy as its flicks a collective V-sign in the general direction of the Glam Rock explosion.

The ritual is briefly enlivened by the Spanish spokesman, who sounds like he's phoning in his jury's crackly votes from a space station somewhere in the Ort Cloud or the Kuiper Belt, but then it's back to business as usual and five points from the Swiss pretty much seal the deal for our superior Swedes. Once the final jury, Italy, slightly mysteriously donate three points to the UK, it's mathematically and musically impossible for anyone to catch ABBA. Which is just as well, as Björn isn't going anywhere quickly in those silver boots.

All that's left now are the formalities. So here comes Sir Charles someone to award the big prize to the winning songwriters. He resists the temptation to say a few words in praise of the bridesmaids and the catering staff and gets straight down to business – though it still all feels a bit like School Prize-Giving Day until ABBA's legendary manager Stig Anderson ambles on and – incredibly relaxed and confident given the magnitude of the occasion – receives his bauble as part of the composing team. Stig, however, immediately finds his claim to be shocked at winning neatly riposted by Sir Charles's priceless off-the-cuff comment that no artist was ever shocked at winning a prize.

Sir Charles wanders off and finds Benny, who wanders on, wanders around and then wanders off again. And now, at last, it's time for the traditional reprise of the winning song. But what a winning song it is. Even more relaxed and more natural than their first highly professional performance, THIS is arguably the moment when we see the ABBA of history just starting to emerge – in the first full flush of victory, a band now more recognisable as the all-conquering, irresistible force and immovable object they would become as the 1970s continued to roll forward.

A mere hour and three-quarters ago they were just another act in just another edition of the weirdly wonderful and wonderfully weird institution that the Eurovision Song Contest has already grown into. Now, though, they're on the brink of something extraordinary and have etched themselves indelibly into the very fabric of Eurovision, into everything it represents and into everything it can possibly be.

You can see it in their eyes, I think. They can't quite believe it. And then, that's it! Now it really is all over! Stig hangs on to his trophy. The European music industry has quite a bit of thinking to do. And my future's mapped out for the next forty-three years. And counting.

Thrive & Survive on Eurovision Night

The internet really is an amazing thing. Take social media and all that malarkey. I don't know about you but I just can't get enough ill-informed opinion on current affairs from chippy numpties who feel an overwhelming need to broadcast their worthless views to the world, based on near-zero knowledge and experience.

Perhaps the only thing that's more surprising than the sheer number of people intent on having their 'virtual' say is the sheer number of people willing to listen to them. Nonetheless, like any era-defining, life-changing, world-shaping technological leap forward – such as antibiotic drugs, the Moon landings, Shake n' Vac, sanitising hand gel or the ready availability of Lordi ringtones – the internet really can be an almost mind-meltingly effective force for good in the world.

Take the Eurovision Song Contest. Just as Christmas now starts in September, so Eurovision begins to kick off during January – and sometimes even earlier if Belarus, say, get an adrenalin rush and select a song almost before the last presents have been bought and the first seeds of excuses have been planted for not attending the office Christmas lunch. With around forty countries now participating, January, February and March see an absolute motorcade of song selection machinery emerging from Eurovision hibernation and firing up across Europe and beyond, before whirring into smooth, streamlined, well-lubricated action in some cases, or cranking, spluttering and clanking through a process of Byzantine complexity in others.

Thanks to the internet, it's a process you can follow in forensic detail. No bend, bump, U-turn or emergency stop in the long road to Eurovision need escape your attention. Now obviously, you can always have too much of a good thing (with the possible exception of world peace). So my advice would be to keep a near-daily eye on eurovision.tv, the European Broadcasting Union's official Eurovision website, and just dip into some of the excellent fan-generated sites that stalk the contest (almost literally, in some cases). Nor should you miss out on 'live' consumption of a few national finals. Or semi- and quarter-finals as well, if your social life really is currently at the crossroads and you need some visual company while you work your way through that big trifle.

Personally, I've developed a particular soft spot for Estonia's Eesti Laul, which tends to be pretty high quality even if I'm almost invariably left incandescent at the eventual result. But of course it's all down to personal taste. Having said that, it IS pretty much obligatory to follow the sedate progress of Sweden's mighty Melodifestivalen as it pursues its annual run. This is a thing of almost primeval natural beauty as it glides majestically onwards, like a mighty river sweeping smoothly from the mountains through the lowlands and down to the sea, carrying you along on its rising riptide of hope that another ABBA or Loreen may be on the verge of bursting forth, fully formed and armed with the best song ever, from the phenomenally prolific Swedish Hit Factory.

This is the factory where presumably tens of thousands of workers, boffins, middle managers and executives labour tirelessly around the clock, harnessing the very latest cutting-edge Computer Aided Design software and eye-watering supercomputers devouring so much power that the visible dimming of municipal lighting up and down the country can be readily spotted from Earth orbit. And all with the clinical, single-minded Nordic purpose of developing and bringing to market fit-for-purpose, state-of-the-art pop acts who instantly render laughable the feeble efforts of delusional nations who've managed to convince themselves, yet again, that "this year, I think we might have a chance!"

All this is, of course, very different from how it used to be pre-internet, pre-video recorder, pre-Shake n' Vac. Eurovision was very much a for-one-night-only affair. You MIGHT just catch a preview show on the Sunday before the contest. But almost inevitably the time was not your own as your mum absolutely insisted you made that long-promised phone call to thank granny for the postal order at precisely the moment you were about to get a sneak peek at what Vicky Leandros had in store for Eurovision that year.

So in all likelihood Eurovision Night itself would be your very first and very last opportunity to soak up the wonder of that year's crop, although some of the produce growing from the contest's frequently somewhat sterile soil (and typically including the winner, the UK entry plus, occasionally, some other quirky or noteworthy effort) might briefly bother the British charts. 1974 was a bit of a bumper harvest in this respect, actually, with ABBA bounding effortlessly up the hit parade for a stint at number one, Olivia N-J putting down her parasol long enough to make it as far as number eleven, and both Gigliola Cinquetti and Mouth & MacNeal leapfrogging Olivia and vaulting right up to the heady heights of number eight. What a banquet!

Now some people I know, somewhat akin to the Flat Earth Society, the Elvis lives on the Moon brigade and certain backwaters of the Liberal Democrat Party, still steadfastly stick to this antediluvian approach and only sample each year's Eurovision harvest on Grand Final Night itself. Indeed, they often claim to be Eurovision 'purists'. But we know better, don't we? Amateurs. Plus of course the advent, in 2004, of a Semi-Final on the preceding Wednesday or Thursday and, since 2008, TWO Semi-Finals on the preceding Tuesday and Thursday has rendered this kind of Luddite approach completely obsolete and, frankly, contemptible.

These days, I'm delighted to say, it's not a question of Eurovision Night at all – it's Eurovision WEEK. It begins the previous Saturday (if not before) and, thanks to the internet, includes immersing yourself in rehearsal footage, the Red Carpet Event and all the essential behind-the-scenes goings-on. This means that – if you're unfortunate enough not to be present at the event in person – Eurovision Week can still be a genuinely all-consuming experience which will easily bite a whole chunk out of your life with absolutely no effort at all.

To sum up: fail to prepare, prepare to fail and all that. To maximise your enjoyment, the run-up to the Eurovision Grand Final really should begin the moment the last bit of Christmas tinsel comes down, the last indigestion tablet has been taken and that Christmas card from Val and Terry (who you assume you must have met once on holiday but who've left absolutely no imprint on your cerebral tissue) hits the bottom of the recycling bin. Only then will you be sufficiently invested emotionally in the battery of favourite songs and sure-fire winners you've selected from the groaning buffet table spread out before you. And only then will that nervous anticipation during the run-up to the Grand Final truly reach such a fever pitch of hysteria and put you through an emotional wringer of such ferocious intensity that you'll be able to reply with an honest, clear and unequivocal "yes" whenever anyone later asks you the seemingly innocent question: "so did you have a good Eurovision?"

*   *   *   *   *   *

Eurovision parties. Colour and clamour. Individual guests arriving in the national garb of different competing countries they've drawn by lot as part of a random selection process. The endless hum of chit-chatter; the cheery clink of glasses filled to their brims with an impudent Moldovan red that Justin ran to ground at his local off-licence; a portion or two of vegetarian lasagne that Jo kindly brought round but doesn't contain 'normal' pasta sheets as Jo's now gone gluten-free; the constant hum of conversation for which the TV flickering in the corner provides a kind of polyglot mood muzak as Easter holiday anecdotes are swapped, kids' escapades are compared and the merits of utility room extension plans are contrasted. Yes, the sound of happy laughter fills the air, all but drowning out the now mildly intrusive sounds ejected from the TV speakers, which find it increasingly hard to compete with the Good Ship Socialise as it sails serenely along on a gently swelling ocean of craft bitter, cheap lager, dry white wine, dodgy gin and diet cola.

Stuff all that!

Rule One of Eurovision. Never, ever, EVER share your Eurovision Night with a non-fan. Don't even share it with anyone who claims "oh yes, we love Eurovision – we watch it every year" unless they can at least have a decent stab at telling you who wrote 'Ein Bisschen Frieden' and 'Dschinghis Khan' and can name at least two Herreys. Because otherwise they will TALK. They will DISTRACT you. They will RUSTLE bags of Kettle Chips, TIP them up to pour the final fragments into their mouths and LICK their fingers loudly when they've finished. Worse than that, they will SPEAK OVER THE SONGS. They will WHINGE about the interval act. They will MOAN about how long the voting takes. They will ASK you for a quick REFILL just as SWEDEN are taking to the stage.

In our house, we came up with a watertight solution to this problem some years ago. We call it EUROVISION LOCKDOWN. No-one enters. No-one leaves. Communications with the outside world are severed. Potential visitors are told in no uncertain terms that their visits will be as welcome as dry rot in a wooden balloon. Friends and family are told not to phone and, if they do, not to expect a reply. Invitations to go to other people's houses to watch the contest are rejected out of hand – and slightly rudely too so they won't bother to ask us again in future years. And on the night itself, the blinds come down, curtains are drawn early and only essential lighting remains on, just to deter speculative callers from ringing the doorbell. (I don't care if they DO need an ambulance.) Eurovision

23

Night should only ever be shared with like-minded souls who want to hear every single song and savour every single moment. In fact, if you do have people round and they've accepted the ground rules up front, I'd still suggest drawing up a simple, legally binding contract of behaviour for them to sign so they know what they're letting themselves in for. It can save a lot of bad feeling later. Although depositing a copy with your solicitor may be taking it a step too far. But I wouldn't completely rule it out.

I've learnt the hard way. On the plus side, we've shared some superb Big Nights with others who worship at the Church of Eurovision – and not least with my very dear mate and former Eurovision hopeful Freddie and his family before they decamped to Ireland, or Ireland-Douze-Points as I call it, showing my age. (You'll have to dip into 'Big Dream, Bum Notes', I'm afraid, for the full mournful story of our pitifully inept failures in the Eurovision entry stakes.) On the down side, though, I've also made some classic schoolboy errors. To be fair, the last one of these was as far back as 2001 when, at some point in February, we were kindly invited round to dinner by friends of ours and, due to the sort of diary pressure that only really happens when you're still relatively young, we had to set a date some way off in the future.

Tragically, that date turned out to be the twelfth of May. And that turned out to be the day when nearly forty thousand people packed into Copenhagen's Parken football stadium to witness Tanel Padar & Dave Benton with 2XL stun the home crowd against the run of play and chisel Estonia's name into the rollcall of Eurovision victors for the very first time. Indeed, this was a victory that showed how a hurricane of change really was about to upset the patio furniture in the Eurovision sensory garden and start breaking up the old cartel that had traditionally dominated the winner's podium to an unhealthy degree.

After much unseemly pestering and cajoling, I managed to persuade our hosts to leave the TV on in the corner while we ate at their big table at the other end of the lounge-dining room. Thinking on my feet and spurred on by a fight or flight adrenalin surge of desperation, I'd resorted to putting forward the proposal that, rather than rely on CDs to provide music-while-U-eat, we might just as well leave the telly on as this would actually save our hosts the trouble of having to swap CDs and interchange Bryan Ferry and the Electric Light Orchestra at regular intervals during the course of the evening.

This classic British compromise was, however, totally undermined by our hosts' decision to place me in the one seat at the table that would mean I'd have my back towards the TV. Needless to say, I worked my way through all three beautifully cooked courses almost permanently looking over my right shoulder and intermittently muttering "sure", "absolutely", "very much so", "I agree" and other stock responses – while my focus of attention was centred on the absence of the Swiss from the contest (having been relegated the previous year) and whether Sweden's entry 'Listen to Your Heartbeat' by Friends (optimistically compared to ABBA in the run-up to the show) might snatch another win and see the title cross the Øresund Bridge again, on what was a pretty thin evening from a musical perspective.

Not sure our hosts slotted us anywhere into their All-time Top Ten Dinner Guests list, to be honest. In fact, even to this day, whenever I bump into the male component of the couple in question, the name of an old Loudon Wainwright III classic just can't help popping into my head: 'IDTTYWLM (I Don't Think That Your Wife Likes Me)'. But sometimes you've just got to take one for the Eurovision team, haven't you?

At least I didn't start texting anyone to share SMS-based Euro-banter during the meal. In fact, it became abundantly clear quite early on during the textual revolution that the very last thing you need on Eurovision Night is one or more 'mates' who insist on submerging you with a never-ending tidal wave of text messages, usually in pale imitation of the pearly witticisms dispensed by the late, great Sir Terry Wogan – and generally not rising much above the level of "well, isn't SHE a comely lovely" and "look at his trousers".

Such distractions from Eurovision really are the work of the devil.

Many times a friend, acquaintance or colleague has dropped the bombshell a day or two before the contest – "don't worry, I'll text you during the show!" – as if they think they'll be doing me some sort of favour. And the level of annoyance and irritation they ultimately suffer, when I've explained that the concept of EUROVISION LOCKDOWN most definitely includes text messaging alongside all other needless and unwanted trivia, will naturally range somewhere on the scale from 'modest hurt' to 'mortal offence'. But look at all the tosses I give! Not one single one, I'm afraid, when it's Eurovision euphoria at stake.

*   *   *   *   *   *

That's enough of the don'ts. What about the do's? The trick is, of course, to fashion Eurovision Day and Eurovision Night so they suit you and only you. Here's what suits me...

With all the anticipation and excitement of Eurovision Eve behind me – and with our Eurovision-themed decorations (flags, album/single covers, band/singer photos, 'Copycat' biscuit tin, Conchita facemask on the mantelpiece etc) having been in place since the previous Saturday – I wake up in the morning after a restless night and having negotiated that tricky, fitful Last Sleep Before Eurovision. The morning means music. And to set the ball rolling, what better gambit than three or four spins of the contest's title track: the brilliant 'Euro-Vision' by Belgian electronic legends

Telex, from the sublime electropop album 'Neurovision'. Entered possibly ill-advisedly for the 1980 contest, it finished seventeenth out of nineteen, with only plucky, luckless Morocco (with their only ever entry) and plucky, luckless Finland beneath them. What a joke. A total travesty.

Then it's general Eurovision jukebox time for a solid couple of hours, with all kinds of memory-jerkers, tear-jerkers, foot-tappers and fist-pumpers taking their turn to compete for attention – including a good few 'spins' of Mekado's mighty German entry from 1994 'Wir Geben 'ne Party' ('We're Giving a Party' – even though we won't be).

Next we head out for lunch – and any tenuous link to any Eurovision nation will do, with picking pizza the ultimate fall-back position, of course. But you'll earn more (fudge) brownie points from your Euro-comrades if you can find a fondue, grab a goulash or seize a sizzling Nürnberger Rostbratwurst (an order which can cause a few blank faces at the counter in KFC, in all truth.)

Then it's time to stock up for the afternoon/evening. It's really easy, as there'll be just the two items on our shopping list: Eurovision-themed food and Eurovision-linked drink. Here we can really express ourselves and a knowledge of the origins of cheeses, in particular, really comes into its own more than at any other point in the course of the year. Jarlsberg, Gouda, Port Salut, Gruyère, Emmental, Laughing Cow – if there's any kind of European link, it's in the trolley. Ditto dips, breads, sausages, salamis, crisps and chocolate. Nor do we forget some Icelandic-style yogurt, just to keep it all light...

Two quick tips. Firstly, when you're stocking up, don't forget the non-European countries! Secondly, think creatively. Last year, in honour of Israel's brilliant Hovi Star, we bought some Hovi(s) crackers, which went very well with the Brussels 'What's the Pressure?' pâté we ate while Laura Tesoro was kicking off proceedings with a bit of Belgian boogie. Actually, one of our food-related Eurovision traditions is quite a recent one, dating from 2014 when Teo from Belarus entered his fine slab of 'Cheescake' into the contest. So one of our tasks is to ritually work our way through a small cheesecake between us over the course of the Belarussian entry, at Semi-Final stage and also again on the Saturday in the event of it actually making it through to the Grand Final.

Needless to say, please eat and drink very responsibly and never disdain a low-fat or alcohol-free option. Although starting the evening with a bottle of Bucks Fizz is, naturally, pretty much mandatory.

Back home – and with fridge filled – it's Eurovision DVD time in order to light the blue touch paper and ratchet the day up another couple of notches. Pick a year, any year that moves you. Then pick another. And another. This year we rounded off this magical history tour with a cracking one-two-three from the 2015 DVD consisting of Måns Zelmerlöw's Swedish 'Heroes', Polina Gagarina's Russian 'A Million Voices' and Il Volo's extremely Italian 'Grande Amore', before rounding off the big build-up with a quick burst of 'Waterloo'. Wow! And at the end of it all I could honestly say "it's been emotional!"

Then it's full EUROVISION LOCKDOWN and the next three and half hours see me basking in the majesty of Eurovision and repeatedly saying to myself: "it's here, it's really happening, it's Eurovision again, I think I may actually pass out!" The ritual, of course, includes taking everyone's orders for votes and then spending a good ten minutes phoning them all through from our landline during the voting window. Then, when it's finally all over, when the winner's been crowned and you're left with that feeling of outrage that your favourite has (once again) been inexplicably shafted big-style by the Eurovision family of nations, it's time for the clear-up and for the family to hit the hay – leaving me to seek solace in the internet and the winner's press conference and, hopefully, the release of the full breakdown of voting figures from the Semi-Finals to see who just missed out on the Grand Final and who finished right at the bottom of the pile.

But wait – it's STILL not all over yet! If Eurovision Eve (Friday) is the equivalent of Christmas Eve and Eurovision Day (Saturday) is the equivalent of Christmas Day, that clearly makes the next day (Sunday) Eurovision Boxing Day. And there are plenty of remarkable and rewarding parallels with the 'real' Boxing Day too. First and foremost, you've got the best new toy in the world to play with – a brand new Eurovision! It's what iPlayer was made for. Plus you've got to apply yourself to the serious task of digestively disposing of the leftover food. Just as a traditional Boxing Day breakfast might consist of two mince pies and half a pound of Quality Street (but don't forget that low-fat option…), so Eurovision Boxing Day will require all your finely tuned skills in pinpointing an alluring chunk of chorizo here, a tempting lump of Limburger there and a still-not-quite-stale slice of schwarzbrot somewhere else, hiding under that thoughtlessly discarded and crudely crumpled paper napkin.

No, it's not until you wake up on the Monday morning that you genuinely start to feel like ABBA in the 'Happy New Year' video…

Even the prospect of the triple souvenir DVD arriving in a few weeks can't completely dispel that feeling. You fumble through the day with a metaphorical black bin liner in your hand and a kind of numb desolation overtaking your body – a shattering awareness that someone has just flipped the egg-timer over again and there's now fifty-two weeks' worth of sand (or thereabouts) to slip down from the top bit to the bottom bit before it can happen all over again.

And boy, on that particular Monday morning, that can seem like one HELL of a lot of sand.

Postcard: Saturday 29th March 1969

Let me be completely candid with you. If your nuclear reactor develops a major or even a minor technical fault, I'm probably not your man. Fairy lights – no problem – I can probably do something with those for you. But when it comes to anything containing highly fissile uranium-based fuel, you'd almost certainly be better off looking elsewhere.

Yet for all my somewhat shaky nuclear engineering credentials, I still don't think it's unreasonable for me to expect those who DO have knowledge and experience of such things to have appropriate contingency plans in place just in case the balloon (and half of Western Scotland) is about to go up.

Now it's fair to say the potential parallels you could draw between civil nuclear power and the Eurovision Song Contest aren't particularly extensive. But I'd make this one small exception. Just as we expect those who are responsible for turning highly radioactive materials into electricity for our homes, schools, offices and hospitals to think ahead and do some 'what if' scenario planning, so we might also have expected Eurovision's early string-pullers to ask themselves some pretty basic questions. What happens if we turn up on the night and the venue's been double-booked with a frilly shirted mariachi band? What if hippies are staging a counter-cultural Love-In, Sit-In or Be-In (no really, there was one of those in California) and bring the host city to a standstill? What if there's a high level of white-noise interference in the Ort Cloud or the Kuiper Belt during the voting sequence? Most basic of all, though, has anyone actually thought about what we do if there's a tie?

So let's subtitle this chapter 'Who'd Have Thought It – How Not to Think the Unthinkable' and transport ourselves back to the night when the last of these nightmare scenarios actually came to pass and Europe was left wondering whether the Spanish language had an adequate word for 'fiasco'. Yes, welcome to the notorious Year of the Four-Way Tie.

*   *   *   *   *   *

What better venue for tonight's drama than Madrid's Teatro Real opera house – all thanks to Massiel la-la-la-ing her way to a shock victory in London's Royal Albert Hall last year. Who can forget how she thwarted Cliff Richard with an edge-of-the-Cliff one-point win that presumably got the big thumbs-up from General Franco – and not because he provided the string arrangement (which I'm pretty sure he didn't).

After a big obligatory burst of Charpentier's Eurovision theme, we get a big discretionary burst from a big discretionary organ and our first sight of an awful lot of flowers. Have we somehow stumbled into someone's wedding? If so, this must be one of those pine-based modern churches and we may firmly be in trendy vicar territory. And what's that strange, magnificent thing slap-bang in the middle of the stage? It's big and metally and very Buck Rogers in the twenty-fifth century. In fact, it's doing a very fine impression of a design idea for a next-generation nuclear reactor, possibly making the men in the front row wish they'd put on their best lead-lined Y-fronts. Oh, I'm told it's a metal sculpture fashioned specially for tonight's show by the great surrealist Salvador Dalí. Excellent! He's also been asked to design a logo for the occasion and here's our first look at it. Lips, an eye, a clock – where does he get his ideas from?

There's no concession to the shock of the new, though, from the orchestra, which does indeed look like it's been infiltrated by the church organist, nestling up alongside the glockenspiel. All we need now is an usher. Bride or groom's side? Here's your order of service – kindly make your way towards the front. But there's no fashionable lateness or killing time driving round the block for our hostess Laurita Valenzuela, who passes close to the sculpture as she strides on stage and takes a bow, resplendent in a trouser outfit that presumably hasn't got any form of radiation-proof lining.

Strangely, Laurita seems to have brought a menu with her and she consults it very carefully as, in a range of languages, she says something important – possibly "I'll start with the fish". And here's our initial glimpse of the scoreboard, which looks as if it may have seen previous service on Election Night (although it presumably hasn't had too much heavy usage in Franco's Spain) and proudly fanfares the names of the sixteen countries taking part tonight.

Ah – here's the head waiter in black jacket and bow-tie. Sorry, my mistake, it's the Yugoslavian conductor who's been charged with serving up the first dish of the evening. Indeed, his compatriot Ivan is already on stage, his tightly clipped black beard and highly decorative lapels giving him an appearance that's more TV magician than Eurovision legend-in-waiting. And appropriately perhaps, Yugoslavia's hopes may be about to disappear in a puff of smoke as the song transforms, before our very ears, into a kind of repeat-after-me Linguaphone lesson, with Ivan offering multilingual greetings instantly echoed by three backing singers who look a bit like wine waiters who've slipped through security, infiltrated the stage and gathered round a spare microphone. It's a little reminiscent of that bit in 'The Sound of Music' where the kids flaunt their language skills as they're heading up to bed and the adults pretend to be entertained.

No matter, the well-heeled, well-dressed punters in the audience are having a lovely time. Some, though, may be tempted to make their own entertainment as the entry from Luxembourg trundles on and then trundles off again. Is it the Yugoslavian song only with different words? This might make a decent soundtrack accompaniment for a soft-focus couple running hand in hand through a sunlit meadow on their way to the nearest Be-In, but that's the closest thing to a compliment I can be lured into giving it. My musical appetite is certainly yet to be satiated tonight. Remind me – what time did we book the table for and when does the feast actually begin?

Phew! In the nick of time, here's a lady wearing something blue and shimmering similar to winceyette nightclothes and doing a kind of 'space boogie' that generates a welcome out-there vibe much more in keeping with the late '60s *zeitgeist*. It's Salomé, channelling a bit of Shirley Bassey, getting her smiley chops round the host nation's entry 'Vivo Cantando' ('I Live Singing') and giving us a good sighting of her gnashers as she ploughs into a much brighter and bubblier offering altogether. Bring me the head of John the Dentist! Enlivened by the occasional astutely placed "hey!" Salomé then proceeds to funk it up a little and, in a very nice touch, points straight down the camera lens as if to say "would you care to fly in my lovely Spanish balloon?" The home crowd certainly seem to have their boarding passes ready.

Oh dear. I just had one of those terrible panic moments. You know the one I mean. The one where you're doing something completely different and the words "did I forget Mother's Day this year?" pop into your head. One thing's for sure: Monaco's Jean-Jacques didn't forget it (though I'll bet he still relied on Interflora). And his ode to 'Maman, Maman' ('Mum, Mum') shamelessly plays the sentimental card as J-J, a mere boy sent out to do a man's job, stands there in his blue quasi-Beatles jacket and his polo neck – the latter worn, I'd like to think, as a result of his mother's insistence that he wraps up warm while he's away from home.

The fallout from J-J's *tour de force* is still very much falling out as green-smocked Muriel Day makes her brave bid to put Ireland on the Eurovision map – a map which doesn't include Eastern Europe and presumably just says 'there be dragons' anywhere east of the Elbe. Then we hear a guitar tuning up (it's never too late, is it?), heralding the advent of the Italian entry, and Iva Zanicchi goes in search of a chorus with slightly disappointing results.

Come on. Stick with it! I can see your eyelids drooping. But things are about to get serious, very serious indeed. It's Lulu time! In the Eurovision equivalent of gunboat diplomacy, the UK has decided on a robust, proportionate response to the bare-faced robbery that they think picked Cliff Richard's pocket last year and turned congratulations (not to mention jubilations) into commiserations, lamentations, recriminations, accusations and above all a determination that it must never, ever be allowed to happen again. Not only have we sent another tried, tested, *bona fide*, proper, legitimate pop star into the white heat of battle – we've also armed her with a song whose very title sounds like the report from a battery of sixteen-inch guns sending a warning salvo over enemy destroyers about to stray into UK territorial waters. Even the chorus of 'Boom Bang-a-Bang' refers explicitly to the sort of relentless pounding you'd expect to witness as part of a major naval skirmish (or alternatively at one of those late 1960s Love-Ins in upstate New York). Or perhaps it's just referring to a heart that's set a-flutter by a sweetheart's proximity. I know which explanation(s) I prefer.

Clad in white-flowered pink mini-dress, Lulu delivers a rattling good performance of her concussive classic, expertly enriched by eye movements that convey mild sauce definitely not of a type included anywhere on Laurita's menu. And our Glasgow girl neatly rounds off with a quick "olé!" that lets the home crowd know (a) she's come in peace and (b) the guns will remain silent just as long as everyone remembers to vote for the UK. Job done. I'd imagine Harold Wilson is dialling in from the upstairs flat at 10 Downing Street even as we speak to offer Lulu the Foreign Secretary's job, with a brief that involves finding a similarly neat solution to the Rhodesia problem.

Now it's time for Lenny Kuhr to turn down the heat on the hob a little with her bedsit-friendly ballad 'De Troubadour' ('The

Troubadour') – though currying favour is clearly still on the menu as the Dutch entry doesn't just hurl duelling Spanish guitars into the pot but also stirs in a good dollop of Massiel's la-la-la tactic to help cater for very different international palates.

So we're halfway through. What do you mean, is that all? Have you picked your winner yet? Well don't do anything too hasty because Sweden are yet to have their say. And here's the man charged with the task, the great Tommy Körberg, destined to walk the boards of London's West End as Anatoly in 'Chess' and to fly the blue and yellow flag once more at the 1988 contest. For now, though, Tommy's main priority seems to be to free his mike lead from the muppet who's obviously standing on it somewhere off-camera. But as a nifty brass arrangement kicks in and the glockenspiel gets glocking and spieling, it's obvious that 'Judy, Min Vän' ('Judy, My Friend') is actually a very good song.

Dapper in his dinner jacket, Tommy's really telling a story here and neatly acting out the tale – an arresting yarn of lost love, found love, lost-and-found love or found-and-lost love, I assume – although slightly worryingly he uses his fingers at one point to show us just how small something is. Blimey, Judy, couldn't you have given the man a break? But we get a nice little shoulder shrug too. I'm with you, Tommy – to hell with her. She's not worth it. The song then observes Rule Two of Eurovision (i.e. modulate for the last bit of the song where it's practical to do so – and for that matter even if it isn't) before a nice bit of funky brass momentarily lures Tommy into doing the funky dude bit and we're all done and dusted. That was excellent! That's a copper-bottomed winner right there. I'd stake my worthless reputation on it.

Hang on. Here's a bloke in a longue suit. Quick – stick him at that table behind the pillar and just offer him the tourist menu. In fact, it's Belgian contestant Louis Neefs who's about to tell us all about 'Jennifer Jennings' (maybe a friend of Judy's and, if so, hopefully a little less superficial and cuttingly personal). It's all pretty low key, except when mild-mannered Louis incongruously hurls his hands skywards and grimaces painfully at the start of the chorus, perhaps as a result of feeling a radiation surge from the reactor behind him.

As Louis heads off for decontamination, he's replaced by Switzerland's Paola del Medico – so at least there may be a doctor in the house. Paola's wearing a white mini-dress decorated with red spots (possibly cherry tomatoes from the free salad bar?) as she launches herself into 'Bonjour, Bonjour' ('Hallo, Hallo' – which has just given me an idea for a sitcom). It's thirteen long years since the Swiss last won this thing (it was Lys Assia who did that, actually) and I'm afraid their luckless run is destined to run lucklessly a bit further, despite the song's nice 'New York, New York'-style closing section that's just a big high kick waiting to happen. And I think it's a racing cert to finish higher up than the Norwegian entry, whose title 'Oj, Oj, Oj, Sä Glad Jeg Skal Bli' ('Wow, Wow, Wow, How Happy I Will Be') may actually be a product of that old warhorse, the Random Eurovision Song Title Generator.

Is it 1970 yet? Despite the odd bright spot, this has been a fairly long evening. Not that I'm counting but there are still four songs to go. That's twelve minutes in total – time to boil three eggs, cook a dozen minute steaks or make at least two trips to that free salad bar. And as soon as Germany's jolly Siw Malmkvist has combined yet another mix-and-match approach to language with yet another outing for what must surely be the last remnants of the Common Market's la-la-la mountain, we're into a French entry that's not my cup of tea at all but probably presses all the right piano-led ballad buttons, despite what sounds to my ears like the mention of a pedalo. And at least Frida Boccara (a) can sing and (b) isn't singing about her, my or anybody else's mother.

Looks like I was wrong about the la-la-la's as Portugal find a few more down the back of the Eurovision sofa before Finland head out to round things off in the shape of hand-in-hand boy/girl duo Jarkko & Laura. Jarkko's got a walking cane and a boater set at a jaunty angle, while Laura's wearing a striking necklace that seems to be based on the beta decay of a tritium atom. Maybe she's planning on plugging it into the reactor on her way off stage to keep the lights shining during the voting. As for the song, well there's only so much that clicky percussion and half-hearted dance moves can salvage as it creeps towards closure and we can comfort ourselves with the thought that soon, yes very, very soon, we'll all be able to carry on with our lives.

*　　*　　*　　*　　*　　*

Laurita's back with the menu. If we're talking puddings, just the profiteroles for me, please. And while I'm considering those prospective full-fat delights that are sure to leave my artery walls looking like a kettle element in urgent need of descaling, I'll enjoy the 'Four Elements' film montage that'll give the national juries more than enough time to stitch up Lulu. Yes, we're treated to lots of shots of lava, golf courses, windmills, lava, boats, waterfalls, lava – oh and the world-famous Alhambra palace. Very nice. It's all accompanied by a very 'modern' soundtrack that makes copious use of that glocking glockenspiel. Indeed, it sounds like the incidental music from one of those late 1960s haunted house movies, where the heroine manages to unravel the real reason for all the poltergeist activity and eventually ensures that the restless spirits can now find peace – but not until she's gone topless a few times. Just to add to the mood, we even get a bit of spooky organ music before a shot of some balloons signifies the end of the sequence. Great. Now Europe can crack on with the real business of the evening – shafting the British.

Only joking, though, because our old friend Clifford Brown is on hand to ensure everything unfolds with fastidious fair play. Indeed, Clifford's got his game face on having, by the look of it, booked a table for five for himself and his team of bean counters. So, as per usual, it's ten points in total for each country to dole out and the first point of the evening goes to Luxembourg, courtesy of Yugoslavia, before the UK and Switzerland gratefully receive two each and Germany trump them all with three. But when Luxembourg give Lulu a mighty four marks and the UK establish a decent early lead, Laurita for some reason gets a fit of the giggles. Maybe someone's tipped her the wink that Spain are about to give the UK absolutely sod all and, indeed, she's still got the giggles after the dirty deed has been done. But Clifford's in no mood for messing about and, much like a schoolteacher makes you keep reading it out until you read it out properly, he insists on the Spanish spokesman running through all the marks again.

Nor are there any UK points from Monaco (don't know why – we've got mothers too) and they go and compound the sin by awarding three each to Luxembourg and Spain, bringing both countries level with Lulu and briefly waking the crowd up. Again, however, Clifford cuts through the nonsense and makes them repeat the process. But as more and more juries declare, it looks like we could have a two-horse race on our hands. Yes, with just three sets of points now left to be awarded, the UK and France are locked together on sixteen, with Spain a couple further back on fourteen. Then France throw in a right old googly by delivering a bulk order of six to the Netherlands, with two of the scraps going to Spain and none at all to the UK. Portugal drag Spain up to eighteen and extend the same favour to France, locking them both alongside the Dutch but just one ahead of the UK, who only get one point despite centuries of bilateral Anglo-Portuguese co-operation.

Appropriately enough, it's left to the Finnish to finish off the voting. Three for Ireland. One for Italy. Just one for the UK, dragging Lulu level with France, Spain and the Netherlands but with five marks still to distribute! What's this? It's three for the Swedes! But they're still very much at the wrong end of the table and it's all become clear now – Tommy Körberg's finger move must simply have been him prophesying the paltry size of the vote for Sweden tonight. So I'll let Judy off. But what a total voting travesty!

Putting that to one side, the really big, huge, massive question is: where are the last two points of the evening going to go? Which of Lulu's rivals will bag them and snatch victory? Answer: none of them! It's the Swiss who receive both of the points, leaving the final scoreboard showing a blanket finish in the shape of a barely believable four-way tie.

Clifford!!! HELLLLLLLLP! How do we split them? What's our back-up plan? Help Laurita out here. She's all a-fluster! Penalty shoot-out? Nearest the bull? (This is Spain after all.) Scissors, paper, rock, lava? ANYTHING!!! Or perhaps each contestant could try to decommission the nuclear reactor and we could see who's left at the end of the evening.

But no, Clifford's voice is the cool embodiment of science and the icy laws of pure mathematics – and there's absolutely no room for sentiment. We have four winners, he confirms in French. "But seriously, though..." Laurita's look of discombobulation seems to say, whereupon Clifford calmly responds to her more or less along the lines of "how many parts of 'four winners' don't you understand?" And before you know it, the splendidly overdressed Massiel strides on stage to milk her last few moments as reigning Eurovision champion and make the presentation. Which begs the obvious question: have they got enough trophies? The answer seems to be yes, so presumably someone, somewhere foresaw such an eventuality and our winning quartet all seem justifiably pleased, even if the overall effect is a little like one of those school Sports Days where EVERYONE gets a prize. I wonder if the other twelve contestants all got a nice sticker saying 'I tried very hard'?

Laurita, bless her, is still trying to come to terms with what's happened here this evening but there's no going back and it's time to reprise the winning songs – all four of them, all the way through, with the respective conductors exchanging the baton like 4 x 400 metres relay runners. Overall, though, as the winners shuffle on and off the stage again, it basically feels as if the last available table at the restaurant has been quadruple booked. "I can only apologise – it's all VERY embarrassing – we've never had this happen before…" Well, at least offer them all a drink on the house!

And as the evening fades away in a fog of anti-climax and the credits start to roll, we're treated to one last, lingering shot of the Dalí sculpture, leaving us to reflect on a curious paradox: how is it that man's ingenuity can tame the power and fury of the splitting atom but remain totally incapable of coming up with a serviceable scoring system for the Eurovision Song Contest? That's a question that some very clever people with a blackboard clearly need to ponder as a matter of some urgency.

Excavating Eurovision (Part 1)

When pioneering archaeologist Heinrich Schliemann took out his trowel and began to excavate the purported site of Troy back in the 1870s, he started (somewhat ham-fistedly) a process that would ultimately reveal no fewer than thirteen layers of settlement at this most iconic and most controversial of ancient sites. In terms of digging up (and, less happily, digging clean through) interesting stuff, he certainly made his mark – although there's absolutely no truth in the rumour started by me that, in Level Seven dating from the Late Bronze Age, he discovered the chord structures that would later form the foundation of at least sixty-five percent of all Eurovision entries. But boiling Schliemann's career and indeed the entire much-respected discipline of archaeology down to a single facile soundbite, I'd simply make this point: it's clearly well worth doing a bit of digging around now and then.

And what applies to the reconstruction of Bronze Age culture in the Aegean region certainly applies to the Eurovision Song Contest. The more you delve beyond and beneath Eurovision's exterior appeal, the more rewarding the whole experience can become. As with everything in life (except pub fruit machines), the more you put in, the more you get out. Yes, I know we all pray for good songs, decent singing, eye-catching staging and human hamster wheels like the one that brought Ukraine's 'Tick-Tock' to rotational life in 2014. I also know how we all love a good old-fashioned Barbara Dex-inspired fashion catastrophe, with the superb Barbara's appearance for Belgium at the 1993 contest doing for self-made dresses what the Great Fire of London did for timber houses built far too close together. (Just for the record, I personally think Barbara's had a bit of a raw deal down the years about this dress business. Her clobber didn't look particularly terrible to me. There again, you haven't seen my wardrobe's spring collection.)

And I'm absolutely certain we all love just a little bit of human frailty and fallibility – for example, when Germany's meticulous recreation of the Golden Age of Swing Jazz at the 2007 Grand Final was slightly undermined by the drummer overdoing the cool and laid-back bit and, all fingers and fumbling thumbs, dropping one of his drumsticks (wooden, not chicken) halfway through 'Frauen Regier'n die Welt' ('Women Rule the World').

But let's head just a little further upstream, pinpoint a heavily overgrown site more or less unsullied by the Eurovision archaeologist's trowel and dig a few test pits to see what we can find down there. So here, in reverse order, is my very own, very personal countdown of the Top Ten essential Eurovision ingredients – all of which can claim to be key components of that 'Perfect Eurovision' I fantasise about whenever I'm stuck at traffic lights, kicking my heels in a supermarket checkout queue or patiently waiting for some genuinely entertaining viewing during an eight-hour charity telethon.

10. Happy Drummers

When it comes to a rhythm section, as with most things in music and in life, I'm pretty much old school. In the world of rock, in particular, I really want my attention-seeking narcissists to be at the very front of the stage, preening themselves and pouting right in the audience's faces, guitar soloing with their bare teeth or effortlessly twirling a microphone stand over their head like a helicopter rotor. Down in the boiler room, meanwhile, the drummer and bassist are charged with the equally crucial task of simply getting on with making the hard yards, like grimy rowers chained below deck in a straining Roman war-galley or like a blameless Ukrainian incarcerated in an oversized hamster wheel. It's simply not a drummer's job to be intrusively and constantly eye-catching or ear-catching.

But at Eurovision what's happening towards the back of the stage is generally well worth keeping a close eye on. In fact, it can sometimes be significantly more entertaining than whatever's happening at the front of it. Yes, right back there in the cheap seats you'll find a whole gamut of unsung heroes about to capitalise on their big moment at the blurring edge of the limelight's glow and doubtless harbouring (i) a fierce determination to make the very most of the next three minutes to inflict just a small dent on musical posterity, and/or (ii) a clear sense of grievance that it really should be them out there in the spotlight instead of that talentless nerk who actually got the gig.

Taken in the round, I'm not sure whether a general edict gets issued every year to Eurovision drummers to cheer up and look happy, whether it's decided on a country by country basis or whether it's a spontaneous decision taken by the drummers themselves on the spur of the moment. Whatever the case, it always cheers me up more than you can possibly imagine to spot a happy drum-kit custodian either at the Semi-Final or Grand Final stage – and I'm sure it'll cheer you up too, especially when you remember to reward yourself for your hawk-eyed observational powers with a small dry sherry, some other tipple or a low-calorie soft drink of your choice.

Istanbul 2004 was a particularly fruitful Eurovision for jocund percussionists. My favourite wasn't even the Estonian drummer who, shaven-headed, horn-haired and scary-goateed, demonstrated an intriguing no-sticks, bare-hands technique that included judicious punching and head-butting of the crash cymbals before, as a fitting finale, sliding across the stage in a kind of crowdsurfing manoeuvre but with the crowd taken completely out of the equation. No, instead I'm thinking of the ill-fated and (shall we say) somewhat limited Latvian entry which like its Estonian counterpart fairly predictably plunged out of the Semi-Final, despite being graced not by one but by TWO happy drummers (underlining the fact that overmanned percussion sections were clearly still an issue in some emerging capitalist economies). To break that down just a little bit further, one of them was just plain-old 'very happy' as benchmarked against the official International Scale of Drummer Joy. But the second spent the entire three, delirious minutes sporting a look of wide-mouthed rapture that couldn't fail to trigger the conclusion that she must have been listening and drumming along to something else altogether on some very well-concealed earphones.

But aficionados of exultant percussion weren't entirely to be denied their Grand Final fix that year, as Belgium's brave entry – Xandee's '1 Life', one of the hot tips for success – was energetically bolstered by an indecently happy bongos virtuoso. Bless him, he wasn't even thrown out of his stride by the unplanned nipple exposure that occurred when one of Xandee's backing dancers had a slight wardrobe malfunction two-thirds of the way through the song.

Hot tips indeed.

9. Falsetto Ambush

Just a personal opinion but I've never really been that big on the Bee Gees. I've no real qualms about the songwriting, so I wouldn't sign up to fifty percent of the messaging in the Hee Bee Gee Bees famous spoof single 'Meaningless Songs (in Very High Voices)'. But I must admit I do generally struggle a bit with the whole falsetto thing and, while I'd readily concede that it has its place in a disco setting, I've always wondered how I might have reacted if I'd been the sound engineer at that historic moment when the Gibbs brothers first road-tested the high voices in the studio. I wonder if I actually might have uttered the words: "are you quite sure about that?"

In terms of Eurovision, vibrating the vocal cords' ligamentous edges (which is what I was told singing falsetto involves by a bloke in a pub, so it must be reliable) can be a highly risky strategy. That goes just as much for 'natural' male falsetto exponents who glide comfortably around the alto and soprano range as it does for the non-specialist delusional who ill-advisedly chucks in a vein-popping, eye-bulging, nut-busting, hernia-inducing high bit near the end of the song for extra impact and possibly as a sign of utter desperation, like a drowning man waving frantically at the people on the beach only to watch as they cheerfully wave back.

Over the last decade or so, in particular, the falsetto option is a tactic that quite a few countries have deployed – perhaps driven by the expansion and increased competitiveness of the contest and the resulting need to search for something distinctive and dramatic to stand out from the crowd. But it's a very fine line to tread. Get it right and the effect can be quite magnificent. Azerbaijan's brilliant debut 'Day After Day' in 2008 – a tale of good versus evil, of dark versus light, of hope versus fear, of doing slightly pervy things with glasses of red wine versus not doing slightly pervy things with glasses of red wine – is perhaps the perfect example. Get it wrong, though, and you'll create a screechy, ear-splitting, somewhat comic cacophony that's unlikely to help you realise your Eurovision dream. However, I suppose it might have some potential value as a crowd dispersal tool or in incidents where the forces of law and order need to flush people out of a building in one of those highly charged hostage situations.

My favourite falsetto moments in Eurovision, though, come when they catch me completely off guard. Sometimes, you can see them heading your way an absolute mile off. That definitely erodes some of the enjoyment. Take Cezar's spirited 2013 entry for Romania, 'It's My Life'. Now Cezar certainly starts off singing in a normal register but what appears to be his Spangly Galactic Villain persona –

principally achieved through slicked-back black hair, a spangly 'evil emperor' high-collared black gown and an equally spangly crucifix medallion – really are a dead giveaway. So it's absolutely no surprise when he effortlessly slides up the scale as soon as the chorus arrives in order to confirm that it is, indeed, his life and that he'll pump out this thought-provoking message in a very high voice if he wants to.

No, personally I much prefer a falsetto ambush. In other words, I always prefer a scenario where a very high voice comes out of a very regular guy who looks for all the world as if he's about to sing very normally. It's like one of those early 1970s horror movies where, at the start, everyone in the village seems absolutely normal. But then the new postman discovers their dark secret and why all the previous postmen kept going missing. Although of course, as it's the 1970s, it would be absolutely impossible to find out the true nature of that secret (which is likely to involve Satanism, diabolism, barbarism and cannibalism) without one or more women aged under thirty going topless. Go figure.

Exhibit A for me, in the falsetto ambush stakes, would have to be David D'or, who harnessed his highly impressive mastery of the very high stuff in 2004 when he only just failed to make the final for Israel with 'To Believe'. It was undoubtedly a technically remarkable exhibition of vocal gymnastics that left me with just one small disappointment: it really would have been the cherry on top of the cake, as the song finally fell away to nothingness, if only David had remembered to deliver his heartfelt "thank you very much" to the rapturous crowd in precisely the same, very high voice.

8. Angry Rap

Are you serious about winning the Eurovision Song Contest? Are you quite angry about something? If the answers to these two questions are 'no' and 'yes', in that specific order, may I suggest a rap-based entry? It'll be the perfect medium to let you get something off your chest while giving you virtually no chance whatsoever of getting within hailing distance of the winner's podium. On the upside, though, you'd have had a chance to vent just a bit of your stroppy spleen and get your adrenalin going. And you can add to that the fact that I'd have been thoroughly entertained. I think that's what they call win-win.

Rap really has had a bit of a rough ride at Eurovision. Even when it hasn't registered especially highly on the stropometer, it's generally struggled to attract the mega-votes. I guess the one big exception would be if you counted Sertab Erener's break-it-down section in the middle of her excellent 'Everyway That I Can' but I'd still argue that she won for Turkey in 2003 despite that intrusion rather than because of it. And that, of course, was a small matter of eight years after rap's first authentic appearance at the contest, courtesy of the UK's Love City Groove with their 1995 entry called, well, 'Love City Groove'. This highly enjoyable number finished equal tenth – so quite respectable in retrospect – and its rap element was decidedly more smooth-groove than angry urban, a recipe pretty much rekindled by Denmark's Kølig Kaj in 1997.

But personally, I want my Euro-rap to have a bit of rancour. Very mildly miffed, like Finland's Waldo in 2009, doesn't quite do it for me. Ideally, for some reason I don't fully understand, I also like it to be in a language I have literally zero understanding of. I suppose if you're that angry about something, it would actually make sense to ensure you rap in English, say, to help you convey the reasons for your vexation as widely as possible. But somehow that's not remotely as entertaining to watch. It's a bit like when you're on holiday and you witness a furious altercation between a couple of locals in the street – you've no idea what they're arguing about but it's peculiarly magnificent. So angry rap just sounds better in Macedonian. Or Montenegrin. Those are two absolutely great, natural languages for rap, as Montenegro's excellent and criminally under-marked 2013 entry 'Igranka' ('Party') only served to underline.

As a result, for me, Ukraine's cracking Orange Revolution anthem 'Razom Nas Bahato' ('Together We Are Many') which graced the 2005 Grand Final in Kiev doesn't quite dine at the top table. Much as I love it, the rapped verses are delivered in English and this oversight isn't really compensated for by the pretty decent level of wrath on display – some of it conveyed by the lead singer, naturally. But even that's comfortably trumped by the two manacled backing singer-dancers who seem genuinely cross about something, with one of them in particular wearing a fixed look of fury that really does seem to shout out: "Water cannon? Bring it on!"

Taking all this into consideration, my *pièce de résistance* in the field of angry rap has to be the shining specimen of this underrated, largely ignored sub-genre delivered by the Former Yugoslav Republic of Macedonia in 2010. 'Jas Ja Imam Silata' ('I Have the Strength') starts off in pretty predictable but nevertheless pretty enjoyable dad-rock territory, as singer Gjoko Taneski interacts with three quite intimidating dancers who are giving it a reasonable amount of slightly inappropriate raunch.

But Gjoko hasn't even had time to complete the second chorus before a proper rapper who's proper scary arrives hotfoot and somewhat unexpectedly on the scene in a sort of rap ambush, his eyes concealed behind scary shades that add nicely to the overall air of gratuitous menace. I can't understand what on earth he's saying but, boy, is he hot under the collar about something. Fantastic stuff. He even holds his hand for a few moments in a cocked and primed fist as if he might be about to flatten the close-up cameraman with a well-timed right cross, before stomping off and giving a proper double 'don't-mess' shoulder stretch as he goes. Even better, we then get quite an angry guitar solo too as the song winds it up still further and arrives at its magnificent irate ending barely in one piece. For some reason or reasons, this storming song failed to reach the 2010 Grand Final. Which, appropriately enough, made me quite angry. But not quite enough to write a rap about it.

7. Singer Hubris

One of the enduring wonders of Eurovision, in my eyes, is the fact that the performers generally hold their nerve astoundingly well under what must be, quite simply, absolutely crushing pressure. They're not just representing their country (or someone else's country, if they're appearing under one of those flags of convenience). They're not just performing in a vast auditorium crammed with thousands of people who aren't going to settle for anything less than a world-class evening's entertainment. They're also appearing live on TV in front of millions of people all around the globe – not to mention the legions of self-appointed social media assassins just waiting to pounce with trigger fingers itching to give each and every Euro-hopeful a good virtual kicking.

If you're going to put yourself up for the Eurovision ordeal, then, a little bit of self-confidence is an absolute must. Any iota of self-doubt will be ruthlessly exposed and ripped open in full view of the slavering masses. Taking all this into account, it really is nothing short of miraculous how few genuine cock-ups actually occur, in terms of fluffs and fumbles. And of course, when they do happen, they're actually vastly more entertaining when they seem to result not so much from a lack of confidence but from a very obvious surfeit of it. It's the ancient Greek concept of hubris in thoroughly modern, musical form – the idea that those whom the gods raise up, through overreaching themselves, are then brought back down again by the same gods as a result of being, basically, so bloody cocksure of themselves.

And what a catalogue it is of those who've fallen from grace in exactly this way. It's a gallery of exotic names with exotic tales to tell – names to conjure with, as they say. King Oedipus, for example. Or King Agamemnon. Or Doctor Faustus. Or Baron Frankenstein. Or Piero of Piero & the MusicStars.

Yes, poor old Piero. I really have got an indelible soft spot for him. Imagine the mountain he's got to climb. He's got to head out there at the 2004 Semi-Final in Istanbul and, with his self-styled MusicStars in tow, really sell his arguably slightly under-powered song 'Celebrate'. Somehow he's got to propel it into the Grand Final and hopefully deliver Switzerland's first Top Ten finish since Annie Cotton sang 'Moi Tout Simplement' ('Quite Simply Myself') way back in 1993. If Piero doesn't believe in his song, who the hell else will?

And indeed, he displays admirable zip, 'bottle' and swag as, sporting a loose pink shirt and a fair dollop of hair gel, he starts by imploring everyone in the crowd to shake it, clap along and, as if that's not enough excitement for one evening, have themselves a really wonderful time. Relaxed and right in the zone, Piero isn't going to leave anything to chance, though, so he's damn sure he's actually going to SHOW us all how to have ourselves a really wonderful time too. To be scrupulously fair to Piero, this can be quite a difficult concept to grasp – especially when you've had somewhat mediocre music washing round your ears and you've just witnessed a slightly surreal Finnish tango number and a very curious (but somehow magnificent) debut entry from Belarus that seemed to be about Galileo and went out of its way to reference the action of Newtonian gravity, if I understood the words correctly.

Wonder of wonders, Piero succeeds absolutely brilliantly in his task right up to the moment a full thirty-five seconds into the song when, having just emitted an impressive Jackson-esque "OWW!!", he nonchalantly grabs the mike stand halfway up with just one hand, lifts it up – and smacks himself in the mouth with the microphone. CLOMP! Oh, Piero! And sadly, though I'm sure this mike-in-mouth moment wasn't the main reason, the Swiss were to miss out on the Grand Final once again. Nothing remained for Piero, presumably, but to nurse his wounded pride as he reflected on the perils of overconfidence, on Europe's pig-headed refusal to have itself a really wonderful time and on its perverse determination to look that particular gift horse in its slightly sore mouth.

6. Pointless Ballet

Long gone are the days when the Eurovision Song Contest was a song contest – when you could simply plant yourself behind a microphone and sing about little birdies and ring-a-ding girls and still stand a fighting chance of success. Interestingly, though, this kind of approach has never entirely gone out of favour and even now, every so often, a country will go for a stripped-down strategy in search of that all-important point of difference that might stick in the memory of the voting viewer. For a classic example, look no further than Belgium's Tom Dice in 2010 and his excellent song 'Me & My Guitar' which primarily involved just him and his guitar. For the classic example, though, well – Portugal pretty much provided the dictionary definition of keeping it simple in May this year, when the most important accompaniment to Salvador Sobral's victorious rendition of 'Amar Pelos Dois' proved to be the absence of just about everything intrusive, eye-catching and distracting.

I suppose you could say that not having a gimmick can be quite a good gimmick.

Generally, however, the contest has seen an increasing focus on staging and performance, which is no bad thing as it adds all kinds of extra dimensions to entertainment content and the evening's overall "did you see that bit when…?" potential. Indeed, even back in those early days when both the contest and, presumably, the world itself was still in black and white, was there ever truly a time when performance and staging weren't a factor in deciding who'd eventually emerge victorious? Think of Teddy Scholten securing the Netherlands' second Eurovision triumph in 1959, singing "'n Beetje' ('A Little Bit', though with no 'Ooh Aah Just' needed) in front of a big picture of a windmill in case anyone forgot where Dutch Teddy and her Dutch song, written by Dutch songwriters and sung in Dutch, actually came from.

Faced with the classic question – how do we sprinkle a little bit of magic dust over our entry in a popular song contest – it's intriguing how many countries opt for a very particular choreographic answer. It's obvious, isn't it? Ballet! Yes, if you're fearful that the attention of the audience might be about to drift, just chuck on one or two ballet dancers to 'interpret' the music and give it a bit of 'depth' (however shallow). What's not to like?

Romania gave this tactic a neat little twist in 2006. As Mihai Trăistariu blasted through the rousing club-style anthem 'Tornero' ('I Will Return') and flaunted his jaw-dropping five-octave vocal range, it clearly wasn't enough to be able to rely on one of the most extraordinary voices ever to grace the contest. Almost immediately he was joined on stage by a plain-clothes ballet dancer who was up *en pointe* before you could say Darcey Bussell and throwing in *piqué* turns like they were going out of fashion. And although briefly supplanted in Mihai's affections by a rival hip-hop dancer and finding her acting skills called on to convey frustration and anger (why didn't she just do a rap about it?), she was soon back out there piling in with the *pliés* before eventually giving up the unequal struggle and joining in with the general clubathon – perhaps leaving Mihai to wonder whether he shouldn't have just showcased his phenomenal vocal pyrotechnics in front of a big picture of a windmill. (They have them in Romania too, you know.)

Indeed, the big prize was destined to elude multi-octave Mihai as he finished runner-up to monster-masked Lordi – a victory providing all the evidence you'll ever need that, when you're pitting your wits against Monster Metal in its most engaging form, even when you're up *en pointe*, playing the trusty old Eurovision ballet card is still most likely to turn out to prove pretty pointless.

Postcard: Saturday 24th May 2003

I've always said that winning's for losers. In my book, victory's very much an overrated concept. Too much effort. Too much hassle. Too many raised expectations for the future. Bumbling incompetence, on the other hand, really ought to be regarded as an art form at least on the same level as contemporary dance. Indeed, bumbling incompetence doesn't just have the potential to be a thing of rare beauty in its own right – it can also linger far, far longer in the memory than sordid success while often representing a much surer path to true immortality.

Think of that archetypal brave Brit, dear old Eddie 'the Eagle' Edwards and his wobbly flopping off the end of all those big ski-jump ramps. And think of how he then trailed in last at the 1988 Winter Olympics in Calgary, Canada – iconic games that also saw the legendary and inspirational Jamaican bobsleigh team go down in the record books as 'did not finish' basically because it was just so slippery out there.

For some reason, bitterly cold weather seems to attract glorious failure like a moth to a very cold flame. The tragic exploits of George Mallory and Sandy Irvine on Everest in 1924 and Robert Falcon Scott in the Antarctic twelve years earlier, of course, still burn brightly as beacons of courage, endurance and fortitude in the face of insuperable odds. And while those expeditions may have ended in disastrous failure, they nevertheless offer eternal, humbling examples of how success can be superfluous when it comes to securing undying fame. But for winners – unlike for Mallory and Irvine, whose terrible but heroic fate was to remain trapped forever five and a half miles up, at the roof of the world, as arguably mountaineering's most famous sons – the only way is down.

To switch somewhat inelegantly from the sublime to the hopeless, failure at the Eurovision Song Contest tends not to be looked on so kindly. Indeed, here's an event where the bottom of the scoreboard really is no place to be, on any occasion. Yet special disdain and derision tend to be reserved for those poor playthings of fate who not only finish last of the bunch but also fail to register a single paltry point on the Big Night. The reasons may be many and the excuses both interminable and gossamer-thin – perhaps the vagaries of the voting system, or technical issues 'beyond our control', or the untimely intrusion of political factors. Or perhaps simply the fact that the song was a sputtering, spluttering dud. But the net result is just the same: the dreaded *'nul points'*. Nil. Nothing. Nada. Nix. A duck in cricket. Love in tennis. A goose egg. A void. A vacancy. An empty space. A hole in time and space that can never be filled. A chasm that can never be plugged. A great big feathery, tone-deaf albatross dangling around your neck forever and a day.

From a *'nul points'* perspective, the first six editions of Eurovision passed by harmlessly enough. But just like the proverbial London buses, you waited for ages and then four came along together. The 1962 contest in Luxembourg saw Austria, Belgium, the Netherlands and Spain rooted at the foot of the scoreboard without a single point to rub together between them, with four more victims to follow them onto the butcher's block in 1963. Oh and in 1964 too. Oh and in 1965 as well. In the Swinging Sixties, Eurovision-shaped failure clearly came in packets of four.

But at least these plucky pioneers who first tasted a Eurovision voting vacuum had an embryonic scoring system they could always blame. Such mitigating circumstances wouldn't apply so much in the late 1970s when the golden age of *'nul points'* really kicked in, its prophet and high priest being Norway's mighty Jahn Teigen, of course. Regrettably but possibly predictably, Jahn's white braces, slightly wonky tie and tight red trousers were individually and collectively unable to prevent him vanishing into the murky depths in 1978 with his spirited entry 'Mil Etter Mil' ('Mile After Mile') – a song which ironically had travel as its theme, though Jahn surely had something rather different in mind than a vertical descent into the abyss of pointlessness.

Norway somehow repeated the trick in 1981, thus somewhat unjustly earning a reputation as Eurovision's scoreless specialists. Because this was actually a weary road trodden by many others in the '80s and '90s, including both Turkey (in 1983 and 1987) and Austria (in 1988 and 1991) on two separate and sobering occasions, with Norway only clocking up a third zilch in 1997. The UK, of course, stood apart from all this bumbling incompetent nonsense, fire-proof and bullet-proof behind its Kevlar-lined musical superiority complex and its pedigree as multiple winners of a contest that was still seen as very much beneath it. Yes, even as the bright new century dawned, *'nul points'* remained the preserve of funny foreigners, lesser nations that hadn't given to the world both association football and the 'f' word, and countries that didn't have on their musical CVs the likes of the Beatles, the Stones, the Who, the Floyd, the Wombles, the Rubettes and the Simon Park Orchestra.

In fact, by the time the Eurovision circus boxed and bagged up its bangles, baubles and beads and headed off for Riga in 2003 – Latvia's shock victory in 2002 confirming the suspicion that Eurovision in the twenty-first century was going to be a very different affair from Eurovision back in the second millennium – no-one at all had joined the Cataclysm Club since Switzerland's Gunvor (NOT Guv'nor) finished a hundred and seventy-two points behind Dana International in Birmingham five years earlier. In retrospect, the preliminary postcard of Loch Ness may have been an omen as, rather eerily, the total number of points secured by Gunvor matched, with mathematical precision, the exact number of plesiosaurs that actually dwell in that (or indeed any other) Scottish lake. And her failure really did only underline the old adage that a white electric violin won't get you very far when you're on the same bill as one of Eurovision's most iconic winners, not to mention Germany's cowbell-ringing, crowd-rubbing legend Guildo Horn, who seemed to have crafted his stanchion-climbing stage act as a kind of homage to Mallory and Irvine and their unquenchable flame – and as an extended middle digit to the Health & Safety brigade.

But change was very definitely afoot. And Riga 2003 was about to see the UK's proud record vanish into a puff of dry ice as Jemini achieved that very special breed of immortality that only comes with lifelong membership of Eurovision's most terrifying and least exclusive club.

*   *   *   *   *   *

Here we are then in Riga and tonight the Latvians have decided to plump for a space theme, principally conveyed through the medium of stop-motion animation and plasticine planets. And to steer us through the best Saturday night of the year, we're in the capable hands of Renārs Kaupers (who propelled Latvia to a healthy third place in 2000 as part of Brainstorm), aided and occasionally abetted by Marie N (who went two better in 2002 with her darkest of dark horse Eurovision winners 'I Wanna'). Clad, literally, in psychedelic furs, Renārs and Marie proceed not simply to engage in the slightly stilted mirth-free inter-presenter banter that literally no-one does better than Eurovision – they engage in the kind of deconstructed, post-modern slightly stilted mirth-free inter-presenter banter that can only confirm the arrival of a brand new millennium.

After a quick video tour of the host city that dips liberally into Marie's family album and reveals that Riga really is the place for you if historic city centres with a rich assortment of gables are your thing, we're ready for some action. Well, WE may be ready, but the show's organisers clearly aren't as there's still time (apparently) to drag out the introduction with a word from the august figure of near-octogenarian Lys Assia, who reminds us from Cyprus that she won the first-ever Eurovision in 1956, plus a live link-up with the International Space Station and a brief word from Sir Elton John in Vienna.

Surely this section could have been streamlined a bit – perhaps by firing Lys up to the International Space Station to sing 'Rocket Man' and thus tick all three boxes at once? She'd certainly have needed to give 'Saturday Night's Alright for Fighting' a miss, though, as that really wouldn't have been in the spirit of tonight's proceedings – especially as the build-up to the event has seen plenty of fun and games provided by Russia's controversial girl duo t.A.T.u., who've allegedly left a trail of tantrums around Riga and done very little to dampen industrial quantities of mindless media 'will they kiss, won't they kiss?' speculation.

Praise be, we're finally ready to roll! A record-breaking twenty-six countries are taking part here in the Skonto Hall and it's very clear that, as this means twenty-six pre-song postcards, Latvia won't be missing any of these gilt-edged opportunities to underline how Riga ticks all the boxes as a travel destination, whether for pleasure, leisure, business, family holiday or weekend mini-break. You'd certainly never accuse them of letting slip the chance to boost tourist revenues, in what is by now standard practice for any self-respecting Eurovision host nation with an emerging capitalist economy to support.

Iceland's Birgitta (postcard theme: modern airport facilities in Riga – tick!) gets the ball rolling with the competent and spritely 'Open Your Heart', which includes a mandatory second-verse walkabout. Then it's time for the night's (intentional) comedy turn: Austria's Alf Poier (postcard theme: a nice zoo – tick!). Now Alf and his beret, surrounded by a small menagerie of cut-out animals, does 'odd' very well indeed and his song 'Weil der Mensch Zählt' ('Because Man Counts') turns out to be a curious cut-and-shut job that solders together a Tweenies-style kiddy singalong with a garage-band thrash. Perhaps more intriguing than the hunted eyes and questionable hip thrusts, though, is the fact that Alf's decided to keep his watch on. Clearly, he's a punctilious timekeeper – or perhaps he just doesn't want to be late for his next appointment with his therapist, which has probably been arranged for early next week, I'd have thought.

Once Ireland have been and gone (postcard theme: green spaces – tick!), we're on to Turkey (postcard theme: historic ruins and a nature conservation area – tick!). Now, it's fair to say here's a country which isn't exactly a traditional Eurovision powerhouse. But they've certainly not held back this time. On one level, Sertab Erener's 'Everyway That I Can' is as Turkish as the Topkapi Palace and, with her belly-dancing backing singers, it certainly has more than a whiff of Ottoman heyday about it. But the song is cleverly modern too and even manages to survive a break-it-down, quasi-rap bit two thirds of the way through without suffering any terminal damage. And as it reaches its breathless conclusion, it most definitely has, as we all like to say in Eurovision circles, gone down big in the hall.

The entries from Malta (concert facilities – tick!), Bosnia-Herzegovina (vigorous Riga nightlife – tick!) and Portugal (bracing sea walks – tick!) don't tear up any trees so it would have been safe to send those artists to the nature conservation area too, but then it's time for Croatia (press conference facilities for all your corporate needs – tick!). Yes, this song is much more up my historic city-centre street. 'Više Nisam Tvoja' ('I'm Not Yours Anymore') is a jaunty number that jumps neatly from Croatian to English at the perfect point in proceedings, all delivered very smoothly by Claudia Beni and five very committed backing singers. The high-octane blond boy on Claudia's far right, in particular, leaves it all out there on stage – which is probably just as well as that's probably the best place for it. And as Claudia's hoisted and held horizontal by her compatriots when the song reaches its closing moments and the blond boy roars his appreciation at the crowd, I'm tempted to say I'll have some of what he's having – if I can get it through customs.

Cyprus and Germany make only a limited impact but now a certain restiveness becomes apparent among the six-thousand-strong crowd. Yes, at last it's t.A.T.u time! Will they, won't they? Can they, can't they? Should they, shouldn't they? Sing in tune, I mean. Well the answer's somewhat equivocal, shall we say, but the song 'Ne Ver', Ne Boisia' ('Don't Believe, Don't Be Afraid') certainly has a decent contemporary sound to it, even though the girls have gone for a t-shirt-and-jeans look which gives the entry a school home-clothes day feel. But we all make it to the end of the song without major mishap before Spain (gables again – tick!) send out their singer, although by the look of her she might be the Portuguese singer again but with her hair tied up.

Israel come and go, garnished with Britney-esque backing singers in garb clearly hailing from a disreputable girls' school that must be a certainty to go into special measures, followed by the Netherlands' springy little song 'One More Night'. Then it's time for the UK to strut their stuff. But after the professional polish of the Dutch, you'd be hard-pressed to see your face in the surface of this one. Jemini's 'Cry Baby' is pretty lacklustre, in all honesty, kicked off by a classical guitar break of the sort that's already been done tonight by Cyprus and Spain, and with vocals that just aren't cutting the mustard or any other type of table condiment. And the male half of the duo seems to have received the same dress-down email as the t.A.T.u. girls. All in all, it's substantially less than whelming. So it's probably a good job we can rest easy in the knowledge that, in the entire history of Eurovision, no entry sung in English has ever failed to register on the scoreboard. That's all right then.

But wait – here's a little bit of Eurovision history unfolding right now, right before our eyes! Ukraine's first-ever appearance at the contest may be a little limited musically speaking but you'd have to give it full marks for including a gratuitous spinning girl in a box. Then it's Greece – though it may very well be the Portuguese singer yet again, on a productivity bonus and putting in her third stint of the evening – before the heir of Jahn Teigen takes to the stage for Norway with a rather doleful piano-led ballad. He uses the ballad as an opportunity to tell us repeatedly that he loves a certain girl who apparently hails from what he says is a beautiful world (and to be brutally honest, quite possibly an imaginary one) but he's adamant that he's not fearful of moving on. And personally, I'd be genuinely grateful if he did – and a bit quicker than that as well.

No time to catch your breath – this is Eurovision, after all – and the hits and the misses just keep on coming. But trust the French (sandy Baltic beach – tick!) to ruin everything. In a brazen bit of cheating, they seem to have broken ranks and, in the shape of the semi-majestic 'Monts et Merveilles' ('Mountains and Marvels'), they've brought along a proper song. What's even more outrageous is the fact that singer Louisa Baïleche has clearly done this sort of thing before – possibly even for a living. Ha! See how far this sort of gamesmanship gets you, France! Then we just need to negotiate Poland (functioning port facilities at Riga – tick!) before we arrive at the traditional rapturous reception for the host country's entry.

Yes, it's the Latvian song (radio telescope you're apparently allowed to climb up – tick!) and, showing a neat degree of joined-up thinking with the overall space theme but with a product placement inquiry possibly needed, they've come up with a little ditty called 'Hello from Mars'. And fair play – this appears to me to be a triumphant, absolutely textbook example of the 'we don't especially want to win Eurovision again this year as it's quite expensive' phenomenon that so many winning countries seem to fall prey to. But is there really any need to make it quite so obvious?

The shocks aren't over yet. Belgium also ambush us with a very decent entry, 'Sanomi', delivered in an entirely made-up tongue as they obviously couldn't decide which one of their three official languages to sing it in. The song's notable for its bold combination of bagpipes, bass guitar and a big squeezebox and it all works out surprisingly well, even down to the highly significant hand actions of the singers, the significance of which is not remotely clear to me. Then it's Estonia and a band who look like they've just emerged from a long meeting at a hip software consultancy and tell us that it's a case of 'Eighties Coming Back', although unhelpfully forgetting to specify which century they're referring to. Nearly there now, and Romania (with a proper modern pop song), Sweden (with a stock '90s Swedish entry just four years too late) and Slovenia (whose song 'Nanana' probably needed to be spelt 'Na Na Na' unless referring to a new genetically modified nectarine-banana hybrid being grown secretly on the Slovene Littoral) enable us to clamber over the finish line in need of a whiff of oxygen, a big foil blanket and maybe even a Mars bar, if it's OK with Latvia.

*   *   *   *   *   *

But before Europe speaks and delivers its carefully weighed verdict – now through the medium of the public televoting system first introduced in 1997 to eliminate the quirks, foibles and nonsenses of the jury system and replace them with a whole new set of quirks, foibles and nonsenses – there are, of course, a few formalities to observe. First, Renārs and Marie return for yet another bout of faltering post-modern ironic banter and then we're fed a quick reverse-order recap of all twenty-six songs. On the upside, this gives us a chance to finally nail down our voting choices; on the downside, I have to listen to a bit of the Norwegian entry again.

To give us all thinking and voting time, we next get a filmed 'music of Latvia' montage featuring Brainstorm, Marie N and a pianist with a parrot on his shoulder. Guess which one of those was my favourite bit? That's all followed by a big reveal of the artists' green room that's been cunningly concealed behind the stage, before meeting this evening's Voting Scrutineer Sarah Yuen, who's wearing a head mike so she's clearly the one in charge here. Sarah also has a seismic announcement to make, certainly at least on a par with the American Declaration of Independence or Martin Luther nailing his ninety-five theses to the door of Wittenberg church in 1517: from next year, the Eurovision Song Contest is going to be expanded to include a Semi-Final as well as the Grand Final itself. Two Eurovisions! Did you hear that? TWO EUROVISIONS! TWO!! EUROVISIONS!!! My hundred and thirty-seven letters to Santa clearly seem to have done the trick.

Iceland are the first country to declare their results, with the first point of the evening going to Estonia and the first twelve-pointer going to Norway. This certainly won't be the only geographically predictable award of the night, as Norway will later reciprocate in kind and Greece and Cyprus will fully match that arrangement in their own timeless fashion that's so popular with the other competing nations. Austria, however, chuck their twelve points Turkey's way and slowly but surely, as each country's spokesperson reveals their hand – though only after fully enjoying their moment in the sun and lengthening an already lengthy old process by vacuous chit-chat and needless nattering – it's evident that this is going to be a tight three-horse race as Turkey vie with Belgium and Russia for the big, big prize.

But soon the evening lurches uncomfortably towards the 'awkward' setting as every sizeable chunk of points awarded to Russia finds itself greeted by the sort of crowd booing and jeering usually reserved for the traditional Greco-Cypriot Mutual Admiration & Co-operation Pact. And this Russia-centric restiveness certainly isn't helped when the Russian spokeswoman reveals that her country's votes have been determined not by a nice plebby, grubby televote but by a hand-picked jury whose existence seems a stark throwback to the bad old days of Eurovision's pre-1997 *ancien régime*.

All in all, then, there's a hell of a lot going on at the top of the scoreboard. But oh-oh... there's a hell of a lot going on down at the very bottom of the scoreboard too. That's if the awarding of no points whatsoever both to the UK and to Latvia (who've clearly overplayed their tactical 'we don't want to win again this year' ploy) can technically be categorised as a lot going on. Nor do Spain come to the UK's rescue as their points are read out by a spokeswoman who, yet again, appears to be the ubiquitous Portuguese singer.

A Turkey-Belgium-Russia photo-finish is still very much on the agenda, however, and Sertab in the green room is clearly excited. You can tell this because she tells the interviewer she's excited not once but twice and the interviewer duly confirms the presence of "such excitement". And in case you didn't get that bit, Renārs underlines that it's all really exciting. To be fair, though, the tension is becoming UNBEARABLE and I very definitely AM excited. Such excitement.

On we rumble. I'm not sure what the collective noun is for a big bunch of national Eurovision spokespersons – an 'embarrassment' perhaps – but like the endless Russian steppes, they seem to go on forever. More unsavoury boos for Russia. More sod all for Britain. But at least Latvia are keeping us company down there below the salt. And here indeed are the Latvian results, with their spokesman sporting the best jacket of the evening and a 'nice' gold necktie as he awards the marks that put Belgium nineteen points clear and very nearly out of sight. But the Belgian results follow immediately and, as they can't vote for themselves, their awarding of seven points to Russia and twelve to Turkey immediately tightens up the race and we're back to square one again. Blimey, this finish is going to be tighter than an ill-judged gold necktie.

And then it happens. Yes. 'It'. Eurovision Armageddon.

Whatever the worst is that can possibly happen at the Eurovision Song Contest has indeed just happened to the UK. Estonia's impeccable good neighbourliness sees five points dispatched by a convoy of trucks over the border to Latvia and this thoughtful step leaves Jemini high, dry, adrift and marooned at the bottom of the scoreboard with the square root of diddly squat to their name. But in other news, Belgium soon find themselves breaking comfortably clear again, twelve ahead of Russia and thirteen ahead of Turkey with just Sweden and Slovenia left to declare. And when the Swedish spokeswoman – eschewing the almost mandatory evening-dress look and opting instead for what might be termed supply-teacher chic – doles out just two for Russia and eight for Turkey, Belgium only need the ten or twelve point allocation to seal only their second triumph in Eurovision history. 'Belgium on the Brink' – someone will write a book about this one day. Not that I'll read it as I haven't finished 'Estonia on the Edge', 'Latvia on the Lip', 'Russia on the Rim' or 'Cuba on the Cusp' yet. Did I mention that the tension's becoming UNBEARABLE?

But no, the Stella Artois is just going to have to stay on ice a little while longer as Sweden unexpectedly give the ten to Germany but entirely expectedly donate the twelve to neighbouring Norway. And the Belgian anxiety levels, which you could cut with a blunt Ardennes pâté knife, is cranked up still further by the antics of the Slovenian spokesman who pretends to leave his station before announcing the final, decisive points. What the hell are you doing? Didn't anyone tell you that the tension has become UNBEARABLE?

My. Oh. My. It's just three meagre points to Belgium! That takes them up to a hundred and sixty-five but leaves them vulnerable to a late Turkish charge. And indeed, at the very last gasp, the souvenir beer glass of victory is cruelly, cruelly, cruelly dashed from parched Belgian lips as Slovenia award ten to Turkey, bringing their total up to a hundred and sixty-seven and rendering the twelve points awarded to Russia completely irrelevant as t.A.T.u. wind up one behind Belgium. What a grandstand finish! What drama! What unbearable tension (did I mention that?)! The crowd erupt as the Eurovision trophy heads off to where Europe meets Asia amid wild scenes back in the green room.

And as Renārs clinically takes the opportunity to plug the Eurovision souvenir CD before fireworks fill the Riga sky, a vortex of despair opens up in the soul of UK viewers as the reality of that distressing blob at the bottom right of the scoreboard starts to hit home. This will be an inquest that points the finger of blame, rightly or wrongly, at everyone and everything from Jemini themselves to the Latvian sound system, all the way up to Prime Minister Tony Blair, who'd clearly failed to factor the imminence of the Eurovision Song Contest into his foreign policy deliberations and controversial plans for military intervention in Iraq.

Sertab, meanwhile, is back on stage clutching a microphone and a trophy, with another couple of awards thrust at her for good measure in a move that momentarily generates a scene like 'Crackerjack' when the kids used to get overwhelmed with prizes during 'Double or Drop' and started spilling them on the floor. But make absolutely no mistake. This is a victory of cartel-shattering proportions, especially following hard on the heels of the victories of Eurovision 'new boys' Estonia and Latvia. Eurovision is changing and power is shifting before our eyes. Some people, meanwhile, would also have you believe that this has been a shattering, pointed and deliberate humiliation for the UK – as if the self-esteem of any nation worth its salt would, could or should be bound up with what happens in a song competition.

And as Charpentier's Eurovision theme kicks in again to round off an extraordinary evening a small matter of three and a quarter hours after it began, poor old Jemini can only console themselves with the knowledge that, as a result of their luckless foray, they'll never, ever be forgotten. But maybe, just maybe, in the fullness of time, they might just be forgiven.

I Blame Sweden

Whatever you do with your life, you'll always be able to comfort yourself with this thought: no matter what disaster, reverse or setback you suffer, there's not a single situation that won't seem a whole lot better as long as you can pin the blame for it on someone else. Never underestimate the value of dodging personal responsibility. Yes, a good scapegoat really is worth their weight in gold. Whatever's gone wrong, it can't be your fault, can it? Why? Because it's someone else's fault. And if they're to blame, then (by definition) you can't be.

Got that?

But this ironclad survival strategy is nothing if not versatile. So it works for the good things in life too. Its main merit is that it completely eliminates any need to justify yourself, to self-analyse, to evaluate, or to apologise for any lucky breaks that may have come your way. If you can build a case that someone else was the main agent in shaping your actions, you don't have to be remotely apologetic or do any of the things you'd have to do if they were a direct result of your own decision-making. You'll be able to enjoy what you do, stop thinking about it – and above all stop feeling guilty about it.

That's how it works with me and Eurovision. There's no need for me to justify the time and energy I expend in pursuing my addiction to it. There's no need for me to defend a decision to stay in and watch the first Semi-Final instead of accepting a friend's invitation to go along to the local arts centre to see some ground-breaking experimental theatre. There's no need for me to find one jot of moral justification for spurning a spare ticket to join a mate to gawp at some low-quality sport on Eurovision Night. Sorry, guys. It's really not my fault. It's Sweden's.

Eurovision is literally my favourite 'thing'. My hierarchy of special times of the year reads as follows: Eurovision; (big gap); summer holidays; (big gap); my birthday; pub lunches; (big gap); Christmas. Yes, as I mentioned a little earlier, Eurovision IS my Christmas. Effectively, that means I'm in festive Euro-mode from January through to June, when the DVD finally arrives. Only when I've fully absorbed the bonus features am I truly ready to move on with my life, draw a line (albeit only a very faint dotted one) under that year's contest and book a summer holiday to help plug the yawning void that's opened up at the heart of my existence. And if you think, in any respect, that all this sounds a little bit weird – well, I'm sorry. It's really not my fault. It's Sweden's.

In everyone's lives, there are some real watershed moments. Naturally, they tend to be the really crucial stuff: first day at school; fourth day at school (mine was a slightly odd school); first, second and third alcoholic drinks; first time I watched 'Shoestring' – that sort of thing. And the 1974 Eurovision Song Contest was certainly one of those watershed moments for me. Now I wrote extensively about all of this in 'Big Dreams, Bum Notes' so I won't bang on about it all over again here. Just to sum it up for the uninitiated, though, watching ABBA win the Eurovision Song Contest triggered a whole chain of really significant events for me, although these did take a good few years to come to fruition properly.

These events largely revolved around gawping at Agnetha and Frida on the telly, creeping incognito into the cinema as an uncouth, unkempt sixteen-year-old oik to see 'ABBA: The Movie' (and in the process boost the average age of the audience by a good five years), building up a secret stash of ABBA memorabilia – plus utterly and publicly humiliating myself when I finally plucked up the courage to blunder into a record shop and buy an ABBA album in such a clammy, stress-packed display of fear, guilt and self-loathing that the girl at the counter was probably counting her lucky stars she'd had a bit of rudimentary first aid training. (The album I bought was 'The Album', by the way. So not just any album. Not just AN album. No. THE album.)

But it's really not my fault. It's Sweden's.

Yes, ABBA's victory in 1974 has a lot to answer for – not least the fact that it didn't just plant foundations for the evolution of a deep love of Eurovision; it also made these foundations so earthquake-proof that they'd be more than capable of withstanding any seismic shock that my future musical evolution might apply to them. So even in considerably later years, when I'd become what's laughingly called an adult, although I might well reach for a bit of Beethoven or Bach, I'd invariably intersperse it with plenty of Bucks Fizz or Björn Skifs.

Ah, Björn Skifs, Sweden's Eurovision representative on two separate occasions. First, at the 1978 contest in Paris, he popped up last on the bill to sing 'Det Blir Alltid Värre Framåt Natten'. Roughly, this translates as 'It Always Becomes Worse When Night Comes' which may, as it turned out, have been a somewhat prophetic title. Mind you, I'm confident Björn and his team would easily have secured a Top Five placing in any Wacky Walk to the Lift on the Way to the Stage competition, as French TV had decided to inject a bit of Gallic creativity into proceedings by including exclusive backstage footage of the sort that really ought to have been held back for the souvenir video.

A fair distance it was to walk too and – following scenes mildly reminiscent of that bit in 'This is Spinal Tap' where the band can't work out how to get to the stage – after finally plonking himself down at his piano Björn felt obliged to offer the audience an apology for his tardy arrival. "Sorry we kept you waiting but here's the top of the bill," he announced with somewhat misplaced confidence as, although he was destined to finish a comfortable six places ahead of Jahn Teigen, boring old conventional mathematics condemned him to end up a disappointing fourteenth overall.

But rubber ball Björn was back three years later with a vastly better song and, presumably, a much better map of the backstage area. The excellent 'Fångad i en Dröm' ('Captured in a Dream') saw Björn again bringing up the rear in terms of the running order (were they trying to tell him something?) but, on the positive side, he'd clearly spent time analysing the reasons why it all hadn't gone so well last time. Yes, he'd pinpointed precisely what had been missing. In a word, gloves. So for his 1981 performance in Dublin, Björn and his entire band took to the stage sporting handwear suggesting that they were perhaps keen not to leave a trail of evidence regarding their Eurovision participation.

The net effect was that of a Cold Case Unit attending a crime scene – and a crime scene it appropriately enough turned out to be when Björn fell victim to daylight Euro-robbery as he barely broke into the Top Ten despite the song being, to my ears, an absolute cracker. I'd even boldly predicted it would come third, possibly subconsciously led by my desire to be able to unleash my diligently honed and carefully crafted 'Björn three' joke. Yes, I know.

Appalled at the blatant travesty of it, I even trekked all the way up to the HMV shop by Bond Street tube station in London's Oxford Street after the contest to get hold of Björn's masterpiece, along with a copy of Emly Starr's equally criminally under-marked 'Samson', which limped home in twelfth place for Belgium. I've still got both singles – give me a moment and I'll dig them out. Yes, here they are. Emly's disc appears to have been produced by someone called Kick Dandy, which I assume was a made-up name although I really hope it wasn't. Björn's song has, meanwhile, transmuted into 'Haunted by a Dream' for this double A-side bilingual release. Tragically, neither record has a picture cover, unlike the copies of 'Let It Swing' by Bobbysocks! and Garry Lux's 'Children of the World' (see Chapter 17) which nestle beside it in my old, much-envied Euro singles pile.

Nor would this prove to be the last time a Skifs disc would be recruited to my record collection as Björn popped up three years later playing the Arbiter on the original double-album version of 'Chess', a musical penned, of course (in collaboration with Sir Tim Rice) by a different Björn and the sainted, bearded Benny from ABBA.

For me, Björn Skifs thoroughly deserves a place in the pantheon of Sweden's greatest Eurovision contenders – not least for having a double shot at the title. Indeed, even at the point when he was vacating the Eurovision stage forever, his country had already long established its status in my mind as the contest's spiritual home. Prior to ABBA's epic win, Eurovision had made next to no lasting impression on me. I think I remember seeing Clodagh Rodgers get her 'Jack in the Box' out of its box and then put it back in again in 1971. And who can possibly forget Cliff Richard's era-defining 'bandy boogie' dance in 1973 as he powered through the excellent 'Power to All Our Friends', which even a fairly buoyant bongos player couldn't lift above third place as Anne-Marie David's majestic 'Tu te Reconnaîtras' ('You'll Recognise Yourself') sent all its rivals packing with a dismissive clip round the ear.

I also have some dim recall of those 'Song for Europe' selection processes where the UK's Eurovision candidate would, on successive Saturdays, commandeer three minutes of airtime on 'It's Cliff' or some other top-rating light entertainment extravaganza and hawk the wares of half a dozen potential UK entries. Having seen them laid out on a rug in front of them for inspection, the British public would then be invited to write in, if I remember correctly, on a postcard or the back of a stuck-down envelope bearing the name of the song they wanted to represent them. Those were the days, to quote Mary Hopkin.

But compared with those opaque memories, Sweden's stunning victory in 1974 stood out clear and bright like a blinding shaft of

72

pure plasma energy against a background of impenetrable cosmic blackness. In fact, it was so bright and brilliant that I almost couldn't look directly at it but had to watch its image projected onto a piece of foolscap paper via a pinhole drilled through a cardboard box. Since those days, of course, the Swedes have racked up a further five Eurovision victories. Now I know this technically puts them second on the all-time leaderboard just behind Ireland's seven successes, which of course included those remarkable four and a half Irish victories in the five contests between 1992 and 1996. (I say four and a half because even in the year Ireland didn't win, 1995, I maintain that the Norwegian song only did so by pretending to be the Irish entry.) But that doesn't, hasn't and never will detract or distract from Sweden's status, in my eyes, as the ultimate Eurovision nation.

Strangely, it took Sweden a full decade to repeat their 1974 triumph, as Björn Skifs and sundry other hopefuls proved unable to match the musical standards set by ABBA. The odd thing is, so too did Herreys in 1984. But they still ended up winning. Only at Eurovision, eh? I'd like to think they carefully considered calling their song 'Water-Loo, Water-Ley' before settling on 'Diggi-Loo, Diggi-Ley'.

But whatever the case, a dynamite combination of neatly coiffured hair, white strides and glittering golden pixie boots proved a sufficiently potent arsenal to dash the dreams of the none-too-competitive competition that year which included Norway's intriguingly named Dollie De Luxe – and despite one of the Norwegian singers looking for all the world as if she was going to try out the old mike-stand-as-helicopter-rotor trick before baling out at the last minute and settling for crossing her eyes instead. Sadly for Norway, 'Lenge Leve Livet' ('Long Live Life') turned out to be a bit of what I like to call a six-minute entry. Yes, it was only supposed to last for the regulation three minutes but it ended up feeling like double that.

Seven years later in Rome, where Toto Cutugno, having won in 1990 with the superb 'Insieme: 1992' ('Together: 1992'), reminded us all just how hard a job presenting the Eurovision Song Contest can be, it was Carola's turn to add to Sweden's expanding catalogue of victories. And what a close-run thing it turned out to be as she dead-heated with France for first place but won on countback having secured more scores of ten points than her rival. I could explain further but, frankly, my own eyes would glaze over, let alone yours, so why don't we just leave it at that? In any case, 'Fångad av en Stormwind' ('Captured by a Stormwind') was a worthy enough winner and Carola gave a vigorous performance, despite her dash onto the stage several seconds after the music had started up – prompting me to wonder whether she'd asked Björn Skifs for directions. It may all have looked a bit 'Peter Pan the Secondary School Stage Musical on Ice!' but I certainly wasn't complaining as Sweden neatly completed their hat-trick of victories and ABBA's legacy glowed just a little bit brighter still.

Fast forward to 1999. Charlotte Nilsson belts out 'Take Me to Your Heaven' and chalks up Swedish victory number four. Not only that, she did it while making only a low-key biblical or religious reference. But two other entries simply couldn't resist the temptation to up the ante in this respect, now that the contest was coming live from Jerusalem twelve months on from Dana International's historic win in Birmingham. The German entry 'Reise nach Jerusalem' ('Journey to Jerusalem') even threw in a bit of Hebrew as part of a kasbah-tinged effort that journeyed all the way to third place, while Croatia found their way to fourth place by taking the fallen-woman route. With a similar 'mystic east' tinge and including a bold reference to crucifixion, Doris Dragović with her excellent song 'Marija Magdalena' ('Mary Magdalene', naturally) may not have won the star prize but presumably she would never, ever want for work in Croatian touring productions of 'Jesus Christ Superstar' if, for any reason, her regular work dried up.

Sweden, then, bade farewell to the second millennium absolutely assured of their top-table seat at the Eurovision counterpart of the United Nations Security Council. Indeed, the Swedes' status as Eurovision aristocracy would easily withstand the thirteen barren years that would crawl agonisingly by before Loreen put an end to the pain, set the world back on its proper axis and repaired the fault in the space-time continuum by blowing away the opposition with the remarkable club classic 'Euphoria' in 2012. And then, of course, Måns Zelmerlöw – with a look perhaps inspired by the casual dress-down code favoured by t.A.T.u. and half of Jemini, and with only animated cartoon characters for company – proceeded to post Sweden's sixth win in 2015 with the awesome 'Heroes'. No sign of an overtime ban at the Swedish Hit Factory, wouldn't you say?

These, then, are the winners who currently inhabit the Eurovision Hall of Fame that's part and parcel of ABBA's homeland. And what of their other entries? How does the saying go? That's right: show me a good loser and I'll show you – a loser. But in point of fact Sweden have had some very good Eurovision losers indeed. More than that, take ABBA out of the equation and none of my three all-time favourite Swedish entries got anywhere near walking off with the ultimate prize. So let me round off this chapter by reaffirming my conviction that Sweden was, is and always will be THE superpower of Eurovision – and by counting down my personal cream of the crop of Swedish entries which, if nothing else, will probably provide you with conclusive proof that I really don't know what I'm talking about.

3. 'It Hurts' – Lena Philipsson (2004)

Now this really should have been a done deal. We'd had Bosnia-Herzegovinian disco. We'd had Turkish ska. We'd had Maltese vaudeville. We'd had Belgian nipple exposure. And now, last out of the blocks in the Grand Final, came Lena – according to conventional Eurovision wisdom in prime position because her song would stay freshest in the televoters' memory as they reached for their mobiles and landlines to give their verdict. That was the logic. But tragically, there's no place for logic at the Eurovision Song Contest and, not for the first or last time, the televoters – who'd replaced the juries' inexplicable behaviour with quite a bit of inexplicable behaviour of their own – activated their genetically programmed instinct to put the merits of the music on 'ignore' and simply vote for their favourite/nearest/mother* country (* delete as appropriate). So for all Lena's professionalism, precision and poise, and for all the insistent catchiness of the song with its classic, almost hypnotic hook, Sweden's hopes were cynically torched on Eurovision's ever-growing pyre of traumatic, tragic travesties.

2.   'The Worrying Kind' – The Ark (2007)

Tell me one thing that's better than Glam Rock. Go on! That's right. A Glam Rock revival! Bangin' tunes, stompin' rhythms, crunchin' 'chop' riffs, joshin' lyrics, preenin' frontman, a drummer wearin' a HAT, plus a beautifully choreographed three-guitar salute to round the whole thin' off – 'The Worrying Kind' had it all, except the support of the televoters. The Great Eurovision Public may not have been much of a fan (the song trailed in eighteenth out of twenty-four candidates in the Grand Final) but I most definitely was. And I've got the signed album to prove it. And no, you can't have it. Or even borrow it.

1.   'Just Nu' ('Right Now') – Tomas Ledin (1980)

Too Awesome For Eurovision. That's TAFE for short. Or how about Sadly Ahead of Its Time. That's SAIT for short. Or how about No-one at Eurovision Really Appreciates Big Kicks Or Leopard-skin Trousers, Do They? That's NERABKOLTDY for short. Pick any one you like, any one at all. Because these three are the only POSSIBLE reasons why this cracking little song, sung by a man who wasn't even put off by dropping something on the floor during his song and then picking it up again prior to leaning nonchalantly on a conveniently placed electric piano, failed to register any higher than tenth place. TENTH? Impossible to fathom when it was clearly, CLEARLY only a tiny bit inferior to that year's Belgian entry, 'Euro-Vision' by Telex, which must surely by now have been SCIENTIFICALLY PROVEN, by SCIENTISTS, wearing LABCOATS, in BIG SCIENCE LABS, to have been the greatest Eurovision entry and therefore the greatest SONG of all time. And in my world that's a scientific FACT!

Postcard: Wednesday 12th March 1958

Growing up in the UK as a music-loving lad during the 1970s, it was more or less mandatory to watch 'The Old Grey Whistle Test'. Tucked away late at night on the nation's third most popular television station, back in the days when the nation only had three television stations and even that often seemed at least one too many, 'Whistle Test' performed a vital service by providing a kind of yin and yang counterbalance to the chart-focused 'Top of the Pops' and by hitting you with all sorts of 'proper music' – some of it listenable.

No, it wasn't all about prog-rock goliaths showcasing their latest ten-minute flight of fancy about pitiless snowfields, the seed of Odin's loins or twenty-fifth century cities hugging the shores of acid lagoons. Nor was it simply about hirsute boogie bands flown in from the United States to batter us senseless with six-minute chug fests about life on the road and girls who, apparently, were either obliging to a fault or having absolutely none of it. (There didn't seem to be much middle ground in this respect.) No, you got some good stuff too. I mean stuff you could sing, hum and whistle at school the next day as you headed into double science and yet another chance to mix noxious pink liquids with noxious blue liquids and hope they might, at the very least, take the varnish off the wooden benchtop near the Bunsen burner taps while emitting a satisfying 'hisssssssss'.

Yes, for me, watching 'The Old Grey Whistle Test' really was all about that sing, hum and whistle test. Indeed, the rather obscure name of the programme allegedly referred to a practice once popular in the music industry that involved playing new records to grey-suited, salt-of-the-earth doormen to see if they'd be able to whistle them after a single listen – the sure-fire sign of an impending 'smash'.

In its first two years of life, this was a test that the Eurovision Song Contest had pretty much failed to pass. To really make its fledgling mark, what it urgently needed was a major hit – a song that would exert a vice-like grip on the public consciousness across Europe and hopefully beyond. Only this would cement the contest's status as something important, valid and thus capable of attracting not only more viewers but also more top-calibre artists and composers. And somehow, inexplicably, for all their merits, early foot-tappers like Belgium's 'Drowned Men of the Seine' in 1956 and Austria's 'Where to, Little Pony?' in 1957 just hadn't done the trick.

But the 1958 contest would change all that. A little Italian song hiding behind a fairly unprepossessing title – 'Nel Blu Dipinto di Blu' ('In the Blue Painted Blue') – would become as close to a standard as Eurovision would ever produce, not just racking up worldwide sales counted in tens of millions and making a decisive transatlantic leap by hitting the number one spot in the US, but also finding itself covered by everyone from Dean Martin to Chico & the Gypsies. Better known to the world as 'Volare' ('Flying'), this mega-smash began its rise to global conquest – and to securing such familiarity that it would still form part of the musical medley which opened the 2006 Eurovision Semi-Final in Athens – on a chilly Wednesday evening in March 1958 when the contest, in its formative years, was still just a midweek fixture.

* * * * * *

We're around twenty miles from Amsterdam in the Dutch media city of Hilversum. All of tonight's black-and-white entertainment is going to be packed and neatly wrapped inside a one-hour, two-tone parcel of song presented by the personable Hannie Lips – by no means the last brilliant name we'll stumble on this evening. And just to emphasise that we're going for sleek and slick, there's not even time for a quick burst of Charpentier before Dolf van den Linden and the Metropole Orchestra strike up the band and I'm half expecting to hear a voice announcing: "tonight, ladies and gentleman – it's Big Band Night – live at the Sands!"

Tonight's tourist menu includes an appetising ten musical morsels for your delectation, with no dodgy British cuisine on show, unfortunately, as the UK's still licking its wounds and allegedly feeling slightly miffed after trailing in seventh last year. (Seventh! SEVENTH!!! In the twenty-first century, a UK Eurovision contestant can expect to receive Maundy money for life and a free set of Jubilee tea towels if they pull off a result like that.)

There's absolutely no mucking or messing around. No preliminaries, no postcards, no facile platitudes, no bumbling banter, no mention of fit-for-purpose airport facilities. Just a polite ripple runs round the modest (unseen) audience and we're straight down to business as the first contestant walks through a doorway and down a few steps, giving proceedings a definite 'Stars in Their Eyes' look and feel.

Yes, in natty jacket and chipper bow-tie, it's Domenico Modugno representing Italy. Hang on, he seems to be accompanied by Fred Astaire – no wait, it's the Italian conductor in white tie and black tails who's going to forgo putting on the Ritz and instead focus on piloting the orchestra safely through 'Nel Blu Dipinto di Blu'. Off we go and Domenico's gliding assuredly through the slow-burning first verse, briefly looking down at his hands before up go the arms and we're headlong into the instantly memorable chorus before down they come again.

No, up they go again – we're back with the chorus – and even the clattering drum kit battered by an unseen percussionist can't knock the engaging Domenico out of his stride as he sells the song absolutely beautifully. Even at this stage, it's clear we've already found our worthy winner and can therefore call off this evening's search. Even better than that, although this perfectly executed song of light and shade is actually all of four minutes long – none of that three-minutes-max nonsense yet for Eurovision – Domenico thankfully hasn't succumbed to the temptation to mention pitiless snowfields or the seed of Odin's loins.

Next down the steps is reigning Eurovision champion Corry Brokken of the Netherlands, in nice long evening gloves and delivering the evening's second highly assured performance. 'Heel de Wereld' ('The Whole World') isn't really a show-stopping number, though, despite a brief Rachmaninov-lite piano interlude. I'm pretty sure the phrase 'back to back wins' is still a couple of decades away from being invented and, on this evidence, it certainly doesn't look like it's going to be needed just yet. But Corry gets the statutory ripple of applause and here's the French contestant hot on her heels and straight down those steps. 'Dors, Mon Amour' ('Sleep, My Love') is a pretty undemanding *chanson* in a 'Born Free' kind of way and singer André Claveau, with regulation jacket, bow-tie and highly expressive hands, spreads his arms wide to emphasise the final note, exchanges a quick handshake with his conductor and then unfussily heads off the far end of the Eurovision sausage machine. The space he's vacated is filled immediately by the Luxembourg entry 'Un Grand Amour' ('A Great Love') which is basically more of the same, albeit with an extended smoulder factor as Solange Berry looks like she might actually be about to propose marriage, or at least some sort of committed long-term relationship, to the main cameraman.

So far, so samey. But now it's time to funk it up a little as Alice Babs, with Sweden's debut Eurovision Song Contest entry, piles down the steps in full national costume and sets out to explore a prime piece of Eurovision real estate: the place we like to call la-la-la land. In fact, Alice has faultlessly delivered no less than thirty-six consecutive la's (yes, I counted) before reverting to her native tongue for the first verse of 'Lilla Stjärna' ('Little Star'). Little does she know that, in doing so, she's accidentally name-checked the song that's destined to dash Cliff Richard's dreams and carry off the prize for Spain in controversial circumstances at the 1968 contest. Indeed, the song in question, 'La La La' by Massiel, will reputedly contain a record one hundred and thirty-eight individual la's (the third-best-known least-known Eurovision fact, though in this case I haven't counted them). So Alice's efforts now look a touch restrained, if anything.

Alice duly disappears off the end of the conveyor belt and next onto the Eurovision baggage retrieval carousel is Denmark's Raquel Rastenni – with proper acting, proper props and everything! Raquel's sitting down and writing something in her diary (presumably "Twelfth of March – did Eurovision – lost to Italy"). And as she gets going with the actual singing bit of 'Jeg Rev et Blad ud af Min Dagbog' ('I Tore a Page out of My Diary') there's just a slight whiff of Miss Jean Brodie about her. In fact, bearing in mind my knowledge of Danish is a little shaky, she may even be telling us she's going to make of us *la crème de la crème* – which come to think of it may very well end up being the title of the 1959 French entry.

Now here's a real highlight as Belgium's singer arrives hotfoot on the scene. The splendidly and thought-provokingly named Fud Leclerc strides down the steps in his lounge suit and we're given a quick, gratuitous flash of a harp before he launches confidently into 'Ma Petite Chatte' ('My Little Sweetie'). Two years ago, Fud's 'Messieurs les Noyés de la Seine' ('Drowned Men of the Seine') gave him his first outing on the Eurovision stage. But one of the key questions now is, do you like Fud's fingers? Because finger walking and finger clicking both feature prominently and we even get a Fud shrug before Fud runs a hand over his hair. He's certainly telling a story, though it's hard to say whether he's trying to portray Fud in heaven or Fud in the other one. Say what you like but Fud's no dud and he's clearly got the best hands of the evening, so his bid for Eurovision glory can't be completely dismissed. But all too soon, sadly, it's a case not of 'Fud on' but of the other one as the man of the evening finally heads off and makes way for the German entry.

Oh. My. God. The future has arrived! Forget what I said about 'Volare'. Take it from me: this is our winner right here. Germany have not only come up with a cracker of a song, they've also cut through the cosy Eurovision consensus with their entry 'Für Zwei Groschen Musik' ('Tuppenny Music'), delivered by Margot Hielscher who's dressed as beauty queen 'Miss Juke Box' and pretending to spin three records with great big holes in the middle as if she's part of – that's right – an imaginary jukebox. This is ground-breaking stuff! And musically, too, this is genius! This certainly isn't just another soppy old love song. We kick off with the brass jumpin' and with that we're away and swingin'. There's even room for a clarinet break, a trumpet break, a piano break, a trombone break and, praise the powers that be, even a quick tubular bells solo! And Margot caps it all with a cracking final vibrato that's set the course of popular music for at least the next twenty minutes and possibly, just possibly will force us to recalibrate what we even MEAN by 'music'. OK, I exaggerate. But I really enjoyed that. Is it too late to vote?

Oh. Here's Austria. Back to normal. Can't we bring back the German lady? Liane Augustin's song 'Die Ganze Welt Braucht Liebe' ('The Whole World Needs Love') is solid enough but meandering a bit and there's not even a hint of a mention of a rising phoenix; the Austrians clearly still have a lot to learn in Eurovision terms. In fact, the song's meandering so much that it may yet turn into an oxbow lake before it draws to a close. But have I spoken too soon? Things are pepped up in the nick of time by another swingin' instrumental break! Oh. That didn't last long. Liane's singing again.

It's time for the last song already! Blimey! And that means everything's set for the appearance of Eurovision royalty as Lys Assia takes to the stage. (She won the contest in 1956, you know.)

In fact, this is legendary Lys's third consecutive appearance representing Switzerland and her song 'Giorgio' starts off with a bit of a 'Lone Ranger' feel before finding itself regularly punctuated by instrumental passages reminiscent of a Strauss gala. But what's this? We've got a talky bit! And another! And another! Is this the birth of proto-rap? Nuts to your 'Love City Groove'! Are we at the white-hot arrow tip of innovation? To be honest, it could do with a bit more anger. Nevertheless this feels like cutting-edge stuff and overall it's not a bad tune either. Not sure what actually may be happening in the song but I think Giorgio might be getting his marching orders. And fair play to our unlikely rap pioneer – the standard of Lys's performance really is excellent. The only thing that might significantly enhance my enjoyment would be if someone could lob in a bit of ballet that has little, if any, point and if I knew how happy the drummer is.

*   *   *   *   *   *

I hate an unexpected development. Particularly if you don't see it coming. But I probably should have seen this one on the horizon as Hannie Lips pops up to inform us that, due to technical difficulties on the Eurovision network, a whole bunch of countries actually never got to see the Italian entry. Ironic, that, as the only thing I hate more than an unexpected development is some misbehaving fledgling technology. I never did get that cordless digital orbital sander to work. Anyway, Domenico Modugno comes down the same steps again (obviously having done a full lap of the circuit) and we get a very welcome repeat dose of 'Volare'. Hopefully Domenico will remember to charge them double time.

But now, at long last, it's the moment I've been waiting for – a close-up of the drummer. Overall, I'd say he looks reasonably content and pretty well focused as he kicks off the interval interlude. 'Riverdance' this certainly ain't but the Metropole Orchestra do a thoroughly decent job as the distant juries deliberate over the outcome of tonight's contest and prepare to give Hannie Lips a quick tinkle. Each jury has ten marks to spread around and I steady myself for the inevitable bunfight between Italy and Germany to see who's going to carry off the trophy.

First to declare are the Swiss, who give three marks to Sweden before spreading the other seven around with reckless abandon. That gives the scoreboard operators plenty to do as they change the scores jerkily from behind by hand. Next, Hannie asks the operator to connect her to Vienna (I hope she reversed the charges), has to tell the Austrian spokesman to speak up, but then has to rein him in again as he's out of the starting gate like Shergar, away and clear before Hannie can stick a black bag over his head and lead him back to the paddock. And when order's finally restored, it's seven – yes _seven_ – Viennese votes for France which sees them into a very early, very healthy lead.

Germany now and it's five for Fud! But France maintain their lead overall and then, after Belgium have allocated their marks, Denmark indulge in an unbridled bout of Francophilia by awarding no less than nine of their ten to France, with only Fud intervening with his single point to prevent a clean sweep. Thud! The French are well clear. Fud! Belgium are now in third place, with Italy acting as the meat in the French-speaking sandwich. The Swedes then spread the filling around a bit whereupon Luxembourg boost Lys Assia's chances of turning the Swiss clock back by donating five to Switzerland.

But I know what you're thinking.

WHERE THE HELL IS GERMANY?

At least France find it in their hearts to donate two marks to what's now manifestly a losing cause, even though their spokesman sounds like another one who's phoning in his marks from a collapsing neutron star. Perhaps he's holding the phone upside

85

down. Or floating around in zero gravity. But then the night gets a slightly unexpected shot of excitement as the Dutch jury award six marks to Switzerland and haul Lys up to just a point behind France, with Italy now nestling in third place a further seven points back.

With just one jury to go, the decision's right on a knife edge. But as that jury's calling in from Rome, it's not going to be Italy's night after all as they can't vote for their own song. Indeed, the briefly rekindled flame of excitement is cruelly snuffed out almost immediately when the Italian spokesman awards the six marks that clinch it for France and the scoreboard operators get themselves into a bit of a tangle trying to chalk up four marks for the Swiss. There's a quick fanfare, a bit of the Charpentier we were savagely denied at the start of the evening and then André Claveau's back behind the mike ready for his reprise, which is briefly delayed while a passing dignitary gets hauled in to do the honours and hand over the trophy in its attractive presentation box (which is presumably worth retaining in order to maximise the trophy's second-hand value).

And as André does his thing again and tries to persuade us that there really is a memorable tune in there, you'd have to say it's unlikely they'll be singing this one again at any twenty-first century Eurovision Semi-Final. Spare a thought for the host nation too, who've gone from top to bottom of the scoreboard in twelve short months (although with a kind of poetic symmetry the Dutch will make it back to the top of the scoreboard again just twelve months later). But for now it's flowers and kisses all round as the orchestra finally play us out and we head off back into the black-and-white night wondering just what a woman dressed as a beauty queen and impersonating a jukebox has got to do to win a song contest. A total travesty...

On a more positive note, even though the attractions of 'Volare' were similarly overlooked by our oligarch jurors, the 1958 contest has laid down some pretty big markers and helped to secure some pretty seminal Eurovision traditions for the future. Props and costumes, to name but two, are now becoming firmly established as a fundamental part of the agenda.

More significant still, the 1958 contest demonstrates that complete Eurovision travesties have a very long pedigree. Indeed, it provides another great example of a key Eurovision Song Contest characteristic that's manifested itself time after time after time after time. If it's justice you want, you've almost certainly come to the wrong place.

How Britain Got Bad at It

'It' being the Eurovision Song Contest, of course.

And you'll notice that the title of this chapter is 'How Britain Got Bad at It', not 'How Britain Got It Bad'. Because the brutal truth is that, broadly speaking, the UK have never really been in love with Eurovision, viewing it instead with a combination of mistrust, mystification, amusement, disdain, superiority, suspicion, frustration and frequent outrage – the kind of cocktail of emotions that can only really arise from sincere confusion about what Eurovision is, what it's for and what we should do about it.

In British eyes, then, it's a classic foreign policy dilemma not dissimilar from deciding how to deal with a rogue state. And the net outcome is generally yet another application of the default British method of coping with foreigners that's remained pretty much unaltered down through the centuries – which is basically to keep talking at them loudly in English and wait for them to come round to our way of thinking (preferably while recognising our position firmly entrenched on the moral high ground).

The nub of the problem is quite simply this: where Eurovision's concerned, we Brits don't just want to have our cake, eat it and maybe hold a couple of slices back for later in a chiller cabinet. We also want to refuse to share the recipe with others AND get everyone else to offer us a vote of thanks for baking the cake in the first place. So on the one hand, we like to see Eurovision as a bit of a joke and fair game for our famous British sense of humour, and we understand why our brightest and best artists won't touch it with a bargepole. But on the other, as the home of the Beatles and the Stones, we still get really upset even when we stick in an (at best) so-so song that finishes down among the also-rans at the bottom right of the scoreboard. What are these European types doing? Don't they realise they owe us bigtime? Don't they realise it was us who invented decent music?

So are we going to take Eurovision seriously or is it all just a bit of a laugh? Which one is it to be? Do we want to take the money – or take the mick? We can't do both. Call it making your mind up, if you will. Inevitably, though, we kick the decision into the long grass and go on trying to have it both ways. We claim we get the joke yet we still get the hump whenever we're 'humiliated'.

It's a bit like your partner telling you they really, REALLY – no, honestly, REALLY – don't want you to get them a big birthday present this year as you REALLY need to save the money for some essential new patio furniture and, in any case, if they really, REALLY want or need something they'll just go out and buy it anyway, blah blah blah etc etc etc etc. No, really. But when you (not unreasonably) take them at their word and the big day finally arrives, they're just a small step away from dismantling your kitchen and propelling the pieces towards you at head height and with some considerable force too. No, of course they didn't MEAN what they said and you should really, REALLY have KNOWN THAT, YOU BASTARD!!! Yes, to my mind, if you think of the UK at Eurovision as a bit like a needy, high-maintenance girlfriend or boyfriend, you'll pretty much get the picture.

It wasn't always total doom and gloom, of course. That arm's length relationship and that element of mutual incomprehension may always have been underpinning it all, but they didn't detract from the UK's ability to establish itself pretty quickly as a genuine Eurovision big hitter. One key advantage has always been the fact that the UK entry can be sung in English, in a contest which for around half its life (first from 1966-72 and then again from 1977-98, if I've got my dates right) has brought into force rules compelling countries to sing in one of their own 'official' languages.

Now you'd have thought this would give us a pretty big advantage, considering how pop music in the English language has been such a fixture for so many decades in so many other countries' charts and cultures. English, many would argue, is the 'natural' language of pop and rock, largely but by no means entirely thanks to American dominance of the music scene. And indeed I'm sure it's generally helped us in terms of Eurovision, even though we've run the gauntlet and arguably pushed our linguistic luck on more than one occasion.

The mighty Bucks Fizz, Eurovision champions of 1981, are as far as I'm aware the only winners ever to repeatedly refer, in the lyrics of their almost perfect Eurovision song, to someone being taken from behind – admittedly by indecision rather than by any human agency, but even so, your mind can't help wandering when you're listening to a song, can it? Plus of course there was the slightly strange and arguably slightly ill-judged approach adopted by Sweet Dreams at the 1983 contest held in Munich, Germany, where the trio not only flew in the face of Basil Fawlty's famous dictum about not mentioning 'the war' but actually did so on no fewer than four separate occasions as they launched 'I'm Never Giving Up' at the overwhelmingly Teutonic audience. Bold, indeed.

Taken in the round (rather than from behind), there's no getting away from the fact that the UK boasts a pretty chequered record when it comes to Eurovision. Five big victories have been secured, of course, but they're all now receding in time into an almost semi-mythical Arthurian past where fact and fable become intertwined and, we like to convince ourselves, only perfidious foreigners prevented us from deservedly winning the damn thing every single damn year. Above all, as a fallen Eurovision superpower, we look back at those glory days when we usually finished second and occasionally finished first – even though at the time we thought we deserved to fare even better than that as it was our _birthright_ to finish first and just occasionally slip back to second – and we wistfully long for those times to return (while still not taking the contest remotely seriously, of course...).

To use a football analogy, we've become something of a 'sleeping giant' – a club that won everything back in the days when the terraces were heaving, fog permanently hung over mud-heap pitches and wiry players with greasy-looking hair smoked fags, wore baggy shorts and were all called Sid or Stanley, but that now languishes in the lower reaches of the lower divisions, dreaming of what's long gone and of what might yet be again, but fearing that this is 'it' now as an ungrateful, unfeeling world passes us by and somehow, just somehow, manages to cope without us.

So how did it all come to this? More to the point, does it actually matter anyway?

*   *   *   *   *   *

Somehow the first-ever Eurovision Song Contest in 1956 did indeed manage without the UK. (Did you know Lys Assia won it for Switzerland?) But having scrutinised the event from afar and drawn up our plans for conquest – much like the Martians eyeing up the Earth at the start of the HG Wells classic 'War of the Worlds' – we threw our hat into the ring the following year. To be fair, we kept the heat ray in the box and it was more a case of toe-dipping than hat-chucking anyway as the song, sung by Patricia Bredin and economically entitled 'All', only came in at around one minute fifty seconds. Seventh place, just ahead of the returning Lys Assia who'd apparently won the previous year, did nothing to entice the Brits back in 1958.

But thanks (I'd like to believe) to boffins called Frank, military men called Pongo and government types called Algy working round the clock in secret caves chiselled out under the Chilterns, by the following year the UK was ready to return to Eurovision with a brand new weapon of mass distraction. Yes, it was time to roll out

Operation Whistle. Europe was about to come under sustained high-pitched sonic attack from those oddballs across the Channel.

Dual-gender whistling was, in fact, just one of the many high points of Pearl Carr & Teddy Johnson's well-primed and beautifully polished rendition of the appropriately chirpy novelty song 'Sing, Little Birdie' that catapulted the UK into second place at the 1959 contest. And when Bryan Johnson whistled up another runners-up spot the following year with 'Looking High, High, High', it looked as if the UK had found the formula for success and that blowing air through pursed lips was a virtual guarantee of a respectable finish in the idiosyncratic confines of the white-hot Eurovision cauldron.

As it turned out, the UK now felt sufficiently confident to dispense with the whistling while it gathered three more second places in the following five years, even though 'the big one' still proved frustratingly elusive. And when uncompromisingly kilted Kenneth McKellar slipped back to a discouraging ninth place in 1966, with his song 'A Man Without Love' and indeed without all that many votes, it seemed there might be some kind of structural problem behind the UK's persistent inability to take the final step into the winner's enclosure. But a man without love was duly succeeded by a girl without shoes – and even more importantly by a girl with a very healthy pop pedigree – and the UK eventually clawed its way right to the top of the pile in 1967 as Sandie Shaw romped home with 'Puppet on a String'.

Yet just when it seemed as if we'd finally cracked this Eurovision caper, we immediately slipped back into our role as Eurovision's nearly men and – notwithstanding Lulu's night of shared glory in 1969 – the next eight contests passed by without an outright victory and with another quartet of second places to add to the burgeoning haul. The reason for this almost constant denial of our just desserts was abundantly clear, at least as far as some of my under-informed elders and betters would have me believe at the time. You see, certain relatives of mine were card-carrying holders of the 'they don't like us' brigade.

Conspiracy theorists probably before the term had even been invented, there was simply no situation they couldn't post-rationalise, erroneously analyse and add a palpable layer of paranoid cobblers to. So any failure to see the unarguable brilliance of the UK's Eurovision entry translate directly into a lorry load of votes donated by our European neighbours, cousins, trading partners and former mortal enemies could always be explained away very easily – although the precise explanation would naturally vary depending on which country it was that was actually flicking the UK a V-sign on any given Eurovision Night. Yes, it simply turned into a game of Name That Grudge.

Spain? Gibraltar. Ireland? The Easter Rising. France? Crécy and cheese. Belgium? Well they just go along with France. Denmark? Something to do with Alfred the Great putting one over on the Vikings. Germany? Take your pick. Yes, the old Euro-shaft might come in many shapes and sizes but the net result was always exactly the same: a continental conspiracy similar in scale to the faking of the Moon landings and Britain's best and brightest pop stars sent back across the Channel to think again. Expertly choreographed (unlike all too many Eurovision entries) and ruthlessly implemented, it was all part of what we might term The Plot.

Nor was this malign, relentless anti-British collusion confined to Eurovision. The World Cup, the Olympics, 'Jeux Sans Frontières', Miss World, the European Figure Skating Championships – even, many years later, 'Going for Gold' – all these and more somewhere carried the unmistakable fingerprints of The Plot, in the eyes of these particular relatives of mine. I think I was desperate for the UK to win Eurovision and pick up at least a figure skating bronze just so they would shut the eff up.

And thank all that's holy, the 1976 British Eurovision Expeditionary Force, in the shape of Brotherhood of Man, finally bucked the trend as 'Save Your Kisses for Me' posted the UK's third victory, only for normal service to be resumed the following year as Lynsey de Paul & Mike Moran finished an unlucky second with the perky and pert little 'Rock Bottom'. Little did we know at the time – and notwithstanding paranoid suspicions among believers in The Plot that the continentals had deliberately thwarted us at 1977's Eurovision just to take the edge off the Queen's Silver Jubilee and Virginia Wade's inevitable victory at Wimbledon – but this was to mark the final act in the UK's Eurovision Golden Age. Twenty contests entered, three wins, ten second places, a third, four fourths, a seventh and that stray, kilted ninth: not a bad harvest by any means. But now a combination of soil exhaustion, adverse weather conditions and questionable agricultural practices would leave the threshing floors distressingly empty almost without exception for the next four decades.

*   *   *   *   *   *

When you look through the inventory of UK acts who've graced the Eurovision Song Contest down through the last sixty years, one thing in particular strikes you. There's a fault line the size of the Great Rift Valley between the generally tried and tested artistes that we dispatched to 'do a job' up to and including 1977 and the vast majority of those who emerged from the quasi-talent show approach to selecting our entry that's pretty much held sway from the mid-'70s right up to the present day. (Though there has, of course, been just the odd interlude where a proven hit merchant might emerge from the morass of mush or be hand-picked for Mission Highly Improbable.) Of course, it's not just about the quality and experience of our representatives. There have been a variety of other factors contributing to the UK's relative lack of success since the 1970s. A key one, of course, is the contest's steady expansion. When you think about it, no country these days has a right to expect to win the Eurovision crown more than once every forty years or so. So basically that equates to two Eurovision wins for each country for every one visit by Halley's Comet. On astronomical grounds, then, I confidently predict that Lisbon 2018 will be followed up by Lisbon 2058. Please send me a Tweet if I get it wrong.

But there's no denying that the selection processes we've generally relied on over the last four decades have rarely done the UK many favours. Too often (though by no means always) the result has been tuneless tosh, vocals that weren't the sharpest, or uncomfortable rabbit-in-headlight moments as unreasonable expectations have been placed on those without the requisite know-how and stagecraft to pull it off under the most demanding of circumstances. Even de-mothballing a few old favourites and golden oldies to perform for us hasn't granted us the golden ticket. Mind you, on the upside, my Eurovision Guilty Pleasure Warehouse has had to find room for a few more consignments, not least 2006's curious punt 'Teenage Life' and 1990's more conventional 'Give a Little Love Back to the World', which really should have been subtitled 'But Only If They Vote for Us'.

And just for the record, Brexit notwithstanding, I don't really sign up to the 'everyone hates us so what's the point in even trying anymore?' mantra. No, the problem is quite a bit more intricate than that. In my view, it's precisely because the UK _is_ the birthplace of the Beatles and the Stones and because music consumers across Europe and beyond have such high expectations of British sounds that they absolutely won't stand for being short-changed by us when it comes to the Eurovision Song Contest. The higher the expectations, the harder they'll punish us not simply when we fail to meet them but particularly when it looks as if we're not even _trying_ to meet them. Or worse still, when it looks as if we're taking the Scooch.

Maybe it's a miracle that our years of mediocrity have been punctuated by any pockets of competence at all. When Bucks Fizz struck glittering gold in 1981, it may ultimately have proved to have been more an echo of a previous Golden Age than the harbinger of a new one, but it certainly showed what could be achieved by a good song, an infectious hook, an ebullient performance, clever staging and an unforgettable gimmick. Indeed, while the rest of the 1980s may have passed by in a bit of a blur of Vikkis and Rikkis, the patient still hung on in there and was even hit by a further bout of runner-up-itis towards the end of the decade and towards the start of the one after that.

But since poor old Gina G endured the full-on Euro-travesty treatment in 1996 and Katrina & the Waves headed over to Dublin the following year to set the record straight, have a word with Europe and not just wipe the floor with the opposition but disinfect, polish and buff it before rearranging the chairs, changing the curtains and liberally distributing scatter cushions around Eurovision's front room for good measure, the UK has endured two decades of starvation rations. Even the involvement of Sir Andrew Lloyd Webber enabled only a quick upward blip in the overall downward trajectory of our performance graph. From Golden Age to Silver Age and now, it seems, to the Age of Pewter, the UK has seen a steady decline in its Eurovision reputation and a seemingly irreversible relinquishing of its superpower status. And putting the politics of the 2016 referendum firmly to one side, from a Eurovision perspective Brexit may well have put the tin bloomin' lid on it for a few years yet, bringing us dangerously close to turning the 'they don't like us' view of the UK's relationship with Europe/Eurovision into a self-fulfilling prophecy.

But when it comes right down to it, does it really matter? Surely the main thing is that we still get to attend the biggest and best party of the year. OK, maybe now we're the guest who turns up in the naff Hawaiian shirt with the £4.99 screw-top bottle of Lambrusco and spends most of the evening in the kitchen bending people's ears about who should get evicted next from Celebrity Big Brother. And maybe when we finally get to commandeer the sound system, the dance floor suddenly clears amid cries of "who's done that?" and "put the Romanian one on again!" But so what? It's a whole lot better than looking longingly over the fence, periodically complaining about the noise and hoping they're not having TOO good a time over there.

So let's not end on a negative note. If Germany could win in 2010, so the UK could still win in the future. One day. Let's hold our nerve, yeah? And let's just savour one more time that last victory (to date) when US-born Katrina dismantled the opposition with, I'd argue, a winner every bit as good as 'Waterloo' – indeed with a song that pulled off the rather brilliant trick of turning EVERY line into a cracking good hook. And all delivered with the consummate skill that, back in the days of Cliff, Lulu, Sandie, Pearl and Teddy, we took for granted but has now officially been accorded Endangered Species status, despite Lucie Jones's spirited effort in 2017.

'Love Shine a Light' – it could still compete strongly at Eurovision today. Above all, it shows what we CAN do when we put our minds to it and stop feeling sorry for ourselves. Now it's just a question of actually doing it.

Come to think of it, I've got this song about Brexit…

Postcard: Saturday 30th April 1994

What's your favourite Arabic-derived word? Mine's 'azimuth'. Although I'm not completely sure what it means, it looks and sounds great, don't you think? I've even looked it up in the dictionary and I still don't really understand what it means. But if I were to choose a brilliant Arabic-derived word to describe the 1994 Eurovision Song Contest, it wouldn't be 'azimuth'. No. It would be 'nadir'.

As I watched the thirty-ninth edition of the contest unfold in front of me on the TV screen, I genuinely thought Eurovision might be dying. Ballad baloney had come to rule the roost, middle-of-the-road mush was master of all it surveyed and the whole sorry shebang seemed to me to have lurched into a terminal tailspin of aural anaesthesia and safety first. Yes, virtually the entire Eurovision community appeared to have developed a collective blind spot – or should I say bland spot – as far as upbeat, infectious three-minute pop songs were concerned. To my mind, the contest now seemed to be just another bland date, with those responsible only too happy to turn a bland eye to Eurovision's sorry fate. Yes, it really was freewheeling down a bland alley. It's OK. I'll stop now.

I didn't know what was worse – the cosy complacency or the complacent cosiness. The decline hadn't even been reversed by the arrival of seven debutant nations from the 'old east', to add to the three that had arrived the year before (though Slovenia didn't reappear in 1994 as they'd immediately fallen through the trap-door of relegation). Strangely, while such 'new' nations seemed at the time to be simply compounding the problem by generally adding to the sonic sewage clogging up the Eurovision pipework, history would come to show that their advent actually saved the contest – although it would be several years before their energy, zest and determination to use the event to help put themselves on the map and reinforce their sense of nationhood finally propelled Eurovision into a bigger, better, bolder, brighter era.

But the really weird thing about Eurovision 1994 was that, for all its musical limitations, it did actually spawn a genuine musical phenomenon of not inconsiderable entertainment value. It was just a shame that none of the actual entries were responsible for this signal achievement. Have you ever been to a gig where the support act is miles better than the headliner? Have you ever headed off to a festival where a bunch of apparent no-hopers way down the bill end up blowing the big boys off stage? Because that's exactly what happened on this occasion, as the world began its curious love affair with dancers in clicky shoes who'd apparently lost all movement in their arms but knew exactly how to whip a crowd up into near-hysteria with a stunning twin-pack comprising lightning foot movements and a whirl of swirly fiddle and pipe music.

As a consequence, Eurovision '94 would forever be remembered as the day 'Riverdance' was born, rather than as the night when Europe collectively decided to strike up the bland.

*   *   *   *   *   *

For the third year in a row we find ourselves in Ireland for the craic, following the victories secured by 'Why Me?' (a ballad) in 1992 and 'In Your Eyes' (a ballad) in 1993. Of course, Ireland also won in 1987 with 'Hold Me Now' (a ballad) and in 1980 with 'What? Another Ballad?' Actually, that should be 'What's Another Year?' (a ballad). But you have to go all the way back to 1970 to find Ireland's first-ever win, courtesy of 'All Kinds of Everything' (a ballad, basically). I'm sure there's a pattern in there somewhere. And now against the splendid backdrop of Dublin's throbbing Docklands, we're about to see if the host country can add to their enviable catalogue of triumph with this year's entry 'Rock 'n' Roll Kids'.

Yes, this evening sees the thirty-ninth running, no less, of the Eurovision Song Contest. That's one contest for every one of John Buchan's 'Thirty-Nine Steps'. And we all know how THAT turned out for the Germans. But tonight could well be very different as Germany are one of the hot favourites, having had the foresight to bring a cracking little song with them in their hand luggage. But they'll have no fewer than twenty-four rivals to beat away from the winner's podium as we wait, wonder and steel ourselves for what may yet, if things go tits up, turn out to be a crushing victory for quantity over quality.

The Point Theatre is our venue and proceedings commence with shots of a splendid night-time river-borne pageant resplendent with a Viking longboat, fearsome dragons and a big papier-mâché Bob Geldof. And as we cut to the stage itself, Bob's joined by a big papier-mâché Bono, a big papier-mâché Sinéad O'Connor, a big papier-mâché Mary Robinson and...oh but before I get a chance to ID all of them our hosts arrive on a firework-lit scaffold.

Disappointingly, Cynthia Ní Mhurchú and Gerry Ryan look like they might be quite competent at this presenting lark and, once viewers have been warmly greeted in Gaelic, English and French and we've been treated to a glimpse of the President, the Taoiseach and orchestra leader Noel Kelehan, there's barely time for Cynthia and Gerry to remind us that Dublin is a city rich in culture (and therefore rich in major and I mean MAJOR city-break potential) and we're finally out of the traps, ready for whatever the night may hold.

And what better way to start than with quite a scary bald man with a tuft of red hair sticking out of the back of his head. Counter-intuitively, the Swedish contestant is also resplendent in very impressive Native American gear but the 'Dancing With Wolves' vibe is quickly compromised when he's joined by a blonde woman in a black bowler hat. It looks like the oddest blind date ever and the song itself turns out to be a pretty pedestrian ballad. Sweden have clearly resorted to what we in Eurovision-worshipping circles refer to as Last Year's Winner Syndrome. Yes, they've entered a song to win last year's contest (though it clearly wouldn't have), in the same way as generals are always condemned to fight the last war, so we're told. But a quick kiss at the end indicates that the date has been a success and, who knows, perhaps they'll plan to meet up again towards the end of next week for a quick decaf cappuccino and a caramelised onion panini.

Tonight's stage set, by the way, features illuminated skyscrapers in a kind of Manhattan skyline, though I think it's supposed to represent Dublin. It feels like I've accidentally stumbled on an American chat show and the US atmosphere is further enhanced when two MC Hammer-style dancers start hammering away to marginal effect during Finland's entry 'Bye Bye Baby'. It's sung by two underwear-clad girls but, despite the visual markers, it's all pretty low-key and barely mid-tempo. There's a trace of ABBA-esque turning to camera but, coming straight after Sweden, this has been a classic case of the bland most definitely leading the bland.

After a quick postcard of Grafton Street – where you can buy things and eat things, apparently, so that's an eye-opener – it's time for Ireland to speak unto the nations and make their historic bid for three-in-a-row Eurovision immortality. As already mentioned, the song's called 'Rock 'n' Roll Kids' and, after tonight's understated start, I find that hugely encouraging. Time to open up the mosh pit, I think! I'm just waiting for a delirious drummer to get the skins going and a thundering bass guitar to start rattling the inbuilt speaker in my telly, before a wail of feedback and a Quo-like three-chord boogie blast reduces the punters in the posh seats to a frothing, head-nodding sea of sweaty, neck-driven perpetual motion. Bring it on! Let's ROCK!

But what's this? Blimey, it's a ballad! Under a wash of rippling piano, Paul Harrington & Charlie McGettigan spin a sentimental tale of long-vanished youth and lament the fact that they don't rock 'n' roll any more. Well, why not? Guys, you had your chance tonight! Golden opportunity. But no – you just couldn't resist the temptation to gaze upon the Gorgon's head. Ballads…

Ireland's ballad is followed by Cyprus's bouzouki ballad and then Iceland's song which is basically a US-style power ballad that's been left on its energy-saving setting. And now, crikey, deep breath – it's time for the UK entry. It's fallen to Frances Ruffelle to banish thirteen years of hurt with 'We Shall Be Free (Lonely Symphony)', a two-for-the-price-of-one title for a song that hopefully hasn't got bargain basement (and above all, bargain ballad) written all over it. I'm not sure what Frances has got wrapped round her head tonight but it looks like she may be planning to put in an appearance later on at the Council of Elrond.

The intro's promising, though, as the funky electric piano conjures up a mood similar to Stevie Wonder's 'Superstition' and invites suspicions (whisper it quietly) that we may at last actually have a pop song on our hands here tonight. Unfortunately, the hooks aren't really hooking me and the song's just patting me politely on the head when I really, REALLY want it to grab me roughly by the windpipe.

At least the next entry's going to be sung by someone with a pucker Eurovision name. Here's Croatia's Tony Cetinski and he's gone for the double-earring look with quite a trendy-looking black shirt. He's also wearing a nice white jacket – I wonder if they do them in his size? But it's a ballad with a fairly small 'big chorus'. There's a bit of muted trumpet and I'm wondering whether Eurovision's cut some sort of easy-listening deal this year with one of those 'Through the Wee Small Hours' late-night radio shows.

Now come on, Portugal. Help me out here. Hit that perfect beat! No, it's a ballad. Blimey, it feels like the third time I've heard this song already this evening and we're only a third of the way through the contest. Perhaps the Swiss can save us. Oddly, the preceding postcard features an Irish fishing village, which is slightly ironic given that it's introducing an entry from a completely landlocked nation. Apologies for my churlishness there, but I think I'm starting to get just a little tetchy. And I can't deny that the seafood in that fishing village did look very good. But as the Swiss entry starts (it's a ballad, naturally) and someone shouts out something – possibly "any chance of any decent entertainment tonight?" – I too want to shout something out. Something along the lines of "who's nicked the Eurovision Song Contest and could they bring it back immediately?"

Full credit to tonight's audience, though, as they're generous to a fault. And I really do mean to a fault. They're especially welcoming to tonight's Eurovision first-timers which include Estonia, to be represented by Silvi Vrait with 'Nagu Merelaine' ('Like a Seawave'). Hopefully now we'll get a breath of fresh thinking and crisp eastern sea-air to pep us all up a bit. The conductor looks a bit Bon Jovi so this could be promising. There's a drum beat and a bit of electric guitar...but IT'S ANOTHER BALLAD! Then it's Romania (a ballad), Malta (a smoochy ballad with a bit of a 'Lion King' feel) and the Netherlands (yet another blinkin' ballad).

Let me put all this in perspective. Ballads have their place at Eurovision. But for my money, their main job is to provide the occasional shady grove that affords us a little respite from the brilliant summer sunlight. One of their key tasks, of course, is to let you go and refill your drink, grab a slab of Roquefort or head off for a tactical tinkle. But line them up end to end to end to end to end and the result will almost inevitably be an interminable musical daisy chain of mush, slush, sludge, drudge and whiny self-pity.

Quick! Call security! Hit the panic button! Germany have smuggled a decent song on stage without the requisite paperwork! Oh yes. Salvation is at hand. Tunes! Hooks! And hats! Electropop has at long last ridden to the rescue as Mekado (three girls, plus two items of headwear) unleash the instant Euro-classic 'Wir Geben 'ne Party' ('We're Giving a Party'). And the girls may well ask where the party is (as they indeed do, quite a lot) because so far tonight there's certainly been no sign of it here. They even seem to have brought a polytechnic lecturer with them to do fifty percent of the keyboard duties and he revels in this pivotal role as he expertly seasons the whole up-tempo dish with the occasional perfectly placed "oh yeah!" in his pleasing baritone.

And we haven't just got ourselves a happy drummer. No, we've got a happy drummer with a headband and spiky bog-brush hair! And there's even a talky bit in the song! Excellent. No wonder the girls are high-fiving each other as the song careers forward, cleverly placing recognisable English words here and there to act as flying buttresses that can provide structural support for this veritable pop cathedral. 'Wir Geben 'ne Party' – four simple words that signify a foregone conclusion. It hasn't really been a proper Eurovision Song Contest so far tonight – and now it really is no contest. It's a certain win for Germany and the crowd here in the Point Theatre – coiled spring that they are – go wild in celebration of the evening's first danceable dose of proper top pop.

Right. Come on now, let's build on that! Slovakia have sent a band. Amber alert! There's actually a guitar riff! It's a sea of big hair, tassels and leather waistcoats and the song aims for a pretty low-key singalongability that, in any sane world, would lead you to conclude that it lacks a bit of punch. But in the context of this evening overall, it actually sounds a bit daring.

Of course it can't last. Lithuania (a power ballad with leather trousers) and Norway (a drippy ballad revealingly called Duett) reinforce the impression that tonight's Eurovision is a bit like one of those school exams where everyone looks over each other's shoulders and tries to copy one another's work. Bosnia-

Herzegovina's ballad is a bit better, though, with at least a decent attempt at an anthemic chorus, plus a bit of soul and not a bad arrangement, before a bit of gratuitous hand-holding between the man in the double-breasted suit and the woman in the subtle pink number creates the impression that we've just gate-crashed a wedding at a Dublin registry office.

Next it's zither time but Greece's mid-tempo effort lacks a bit of edge. Am I allowed to mention the blunt leading the blunt? Then Austria's Petra Frey brings a message of peace in the shape of a regulation ballad that's prefaced by a postcard showing a golf course and some people playing some golf on it. And with Mekado currently sitting pin high but the rest of the field hacking around in the rough and some even plugged in a bunker, tonight's in danger of becoming a procession – a procession that Spain's Alejandro Abad (with a growly ballad) seems powerless to do anything about. Just four holes left to play.

Dublin's being touted tonight as the city that never sleeps – and at least the snoozefest we're enduring lets you admire the irony of that claim. But hang on. Here's Hungary. Another of tonight's debutants, they've clearly not read the Eurovision instruction booklet properly. They clearly did get the message about the ballad. But they didn't read the bit about it having to be useless. So there's a nice acoustic guitar riff before Friderika Bayer joins the fray with a very decent melody. No, 'Kinek Mondjam el Vétkeimet?' ('To Whom Can I Tell My Sins?') is actually good. Simultaneously simple and clever, with a tidy bit of woodwind, it's like they're actually trying. They obviously need to go and read that instruction booklet again. Try the troubleshooting section at the end, I'd suggest. Then it's back-to-back new boys – Russia and Poland – with back-to-back ballads, almost inevitably, though Youdipph's effort for the Russians does at least tease us by verging on mid-tempo.

I think I'm definitely suffering from ballad fatigue. Surely there must be some sort of local by-law that can empower the authorities here to stop so many ballads assembling together in a public place during the hours of darkness? Can the last song of the evening, from France, help us out at all? Well, yes – *un peu*. In the most leftfield entry of the evening, Nina Morato forsakes the 1974 standard-issue Bay City Rollers cap she's wearing in the postcard for a crumpled velvety black Artful Dodger hat as she delivers 'Je Suis un Vrai Garçon' ('I'm a Real Boy'), a quirky tune based around some quite nice Pink Floyd-y or perhaps Pinball Wizard-y acoustic guitar chords. Not sure the vocals are really on the money but by this point I don't really care, and with a quick gratuitous scream Nina draws a line under the entertainment for the evening. Ho hum.

*   *   *   *   *   *

Or does she? Because while the juries are given just a few more minutes to find imaginative ways of extending The Plot to batter the Germans, we've got just over six minutes to fill. And we're going to fill it with a kind of prog-rock opera in Celtic terpsichorean form. Bill Whelan's 'Riverdance'! Imagine if Yes were Irish, could jump, leap and spin in tap shoes, and had been specially commissioned to provide a folky-sounding interval act for a Dublin-based Eurovision. That's the kind of territory we're in. In fact, they probably had Yes all lined up in case Michael Flatley refused. Or in case Michael flatly refused.

The piece starts in suitably atmospheric fashion with a lovely little choral sequence before a harp ripples, they fire up the fiddles and Jean Butler trips lightly over the stage. Then there's a clattering of big drums and – hey, where did HE come from? Michael Flatley launches himself onto the stage like a guided missile and, with feet blurring and silk shirt flapping, creates an incredible rat-a-tat-tat of tap action like God drumming his fingers on the corrugated iron roof of the world.

106

Now Jean's back, with a change of shoes successfully negotiated, and it's a non-stop cavalcade of click click, flick flick, click click, tap tap, hop hop, click click, swirl swirl. Two become eight, who then become twenty-four, all of them lining up, ramrod straight and creating a seamlessly co-ordinated tumult as if you've just stumbled into the world's biggest field of crickets and somehow they're all in time with each other. Click click, flick flick, tap, tap, hop hop, look look, swirl swirl, click click, twirl twirl, look look, flick flick, click click, tap tap. And then suddenly it's all over. Now THAT's a cheer! And THAT's a standing ovation! And that WAS entertainment... It really was pretty remarkable stuff. Clap clap! Whoop whoop! Where's the bar, where's the bar?

How much more excitement can we expect this evening? Well — none at all, actually. Because it's time for the voting. Yes, the juries are about to test twenty-five separate video links and Cynthia and Gerry are going to see if they can land the Eurovision voting jumbo jet without alarm or mishap on an airstrip the size of a postage stamp. And with each jury having twelve, ten, eight, seven, six, five, four, three, two and one points to award, this isn't going to be keyhole surgery either.

Sweden award the first point of the evening to Austria, before going on to end their sequence by giving ten to Ireland and twelve to Hungary. Finland likewise slip a maximum to the Magyars, but only find three for Germany. Are they SERIOUSLY saying they thought there were SEVEN better songs this evening? But it's good to see Hungary feasting on some just desserts and they secure a third bullseye in a row when the host country delivers them a further dozen points, as well as one point for the UK (to ironic cheers...). But after Cyprus have sensibly ensured that some goodwill can be maintained in the East Mediterranean by donating their dozen to Greece (later reciprocated, of course, because it would have been rude not to), a new pattern emerges as Ireland chalk up fifty-eight out of a possible sixty points as the next five juries have their say.

With their heroes now well clear, the crowd are going absolutely bananas, so I hope they're not planning on tucking into any of that seafood we saw earlier because that just wouldn't mix. Personally, I'm not really sure why this is happening. Do the juries think they're voting for 'Riverdance'? Poland push themselves up into second position as more spokespersons pronounce judgement but Ireland are now so comfortably clear that there's a total absence of tension at the top of the scoreboard. Indeed, with Austria's votes – announced by a spokeswoman aided by a disembodied hand that actually looks like it's hovering over a panic button – the lead stretches to thirty-eight. Time to hit that button, I'd respectfully suggest.

Spain's votes seal it. 'Rock 'n' Roll Kids' crashes through the two hundred barrier and achieves a final score almost twice as big as third-placed Mekado's. So let's get this right – you're saying, basically, that Ireland's entry was twice as good as Germany's? Yeah. Right. But credit where it's due. For Ireland, two-in-a-row has become three-in-a-row and as a slightly stunned Paul and Charlie return to the stage to a rapturous response and to swirl any woman within easy reach, it's probably not worth trying to make sense of it all. It's a night of many milestones – first male duo to win Eurovision, biggest winning margin to date etc etc etc – but will this victory also go down as a bit of a millstone for those of us who see Eurovision essentially as a pop music contest? Has the contest entered uninspiring middle age? Or possibly even advanced old age? Can it survive – or is the craic beginning to show?

Excavating Eurovision (Part 2)

Congratulations on making it this far. You're basically halfway there. In Eurovision terms, then, you've made it to the top of the right-hand side of the scoreboard. And as every aficionado of the contest knows, anywhere on the left-hand side will count as a decent finish these days. But let's not fall into the trap of thinking that the result is what really matters at the Eurovision Song Contest. Victory's a mirage, success is an impostor and, as I said earlier, winning's for losers.

My main proposition, however, is that the more you're hung up on the outcome, the less you'll be able to spot and savour the strange idiosyncrasies, blemishes and other distinguishing surface features that pock-mark the face of every Eurovision and give each edition of the contest its own unique character and charm. And while each one of these features is different, it's still handy to compartmentalise them for easy recall when you've got a few moments to kill – perhaps when your internet provider's helpline is assuring you your call is valuable to them and, just to prove it, they've put you in a queue on hold for thirty-five minutes.

So if, like any good Eurovision jury spokesperson, you could first just eat up a few more valuable seconds by unnecessarily and insincerely congratulating me on the great show I'm putting on, I'll then crack on with counting down the remainder of my Top Ten list of essential ingredients in my hypothetical 'Perfect Eurovision'.

5. A Good Old-Fashioned Shambles

I may have imagined this but I think it was Isaac Newton who once proved that, if you put a man in a completely empty room, within a maximum of four hours he'd have made a complete and utter balls-up of something. One of the less well known appendices to *Principia*

Mathematica, I'll grant you, but let's face it – a classic hash is a thing of profound, almost mathematical beauty. I always maintain that the world would function so much better if we didn't put people in charge of it. And for genuine gaff buffs the world over, Eurovision has a put-your-foot-in-it pedigree to bear comparison with the very best anywhere on this beautiful, fragile blue planet of ours.

One mark of a really good shambles is when those caught at the sharp end appear to be the mere playthings of fate or, blameless to a fault, find themselves unceremoniously hung out to dry by someone or something safely residing far from the public gaze. But timing can be all-important too. So when sister act Azúcar Moreno kicked off the 1990 show for Spain, it was undoubtedly the worst possible moment for the backing track machine to go on the blink, or possibly for the person operating the backing track machine to go on the blink, or both. Now, we've all been there. We all had those moments in our misguided formative years when we popped that cassette with that precious clip of Simon & Garfunkel's 'Mrs Robinson' into our Philips radio-cassette player, only to discover we'd accidentally taped over it with the sound of silence or, just possibly, with the Sound of Silence. (Not the Dami Im one.) And on this occasion, the stage assumed the air of a roll-on roll-off ferry as, after nearly half a minute of awkward aural nothingness, the sisters eventually sauntered onto the set, took stock, gesticulated briefly and sauntered off again while the punchy but late-arriving backing track eventually picked up steam and the guitar player, clearly recognising that it really is an ill wind, took the opportunity to express his frustration and fill the gap with a nifty bit of dad dancing.

But for Eurovision's true mistress of chaos-infused distress we need look no further than Dana International, who (impressively) was at the epicentre of a quality shambles two years on the bounce – first when receiving the big prize in 1998 and then, with beautiful symmetry, when presenting the big prize to her successor Charlotte Nilsson twelve months later. The first of these incidents was the notorious Very Long Wait, when Terry Wogan and the presentation party find themselves marooned on stage in full public view for at least two geological epochs while waiting for Dana to reappear, only to be disappointed as Dana's team eventually turn up but Dana doesn't ("where's our girl?" asks Terry, the unspoken answer being "still backstage slipping into a feathery Jean Paul Gaultier number"). And as, finally, Dana slips across behind them to install herself behind the microphone for the reprise of 'Diva', Terry's left to shout his thankyous and goodbyes over priceless scenes of tumult, fuss and hubbub. Exquisite.

In 1999, if anything, Dana went one better by picking up the heavy-looking trophy and not only immediately crashing to the floor with it in a flurry of fashionable fabric but also taking one of the dignitaries with her, before tottering off stage in a blur of feather burlesque fans under Charlotte's patient but bemused gaze. I don't know. You'd almost have thought Dana International was _trying_ to attract attention, wouldn't you?

4. Leftfield Language Selection

The Tower of Babel. A monument to man's impudence whose destruction sealed his descent into a sea of squabbling tongues, mutual incomprehension and eternal suspicion. But there again, so did the Eurovision Song Contest when it reverted to its 'native language' rule in 1977.

When that was rescinded twenty-two years later, of course, competing countries basically faced a dilemma: stick with their own official tongue (or one of them) or opt for English in a bid to hoover up a few extra votes. There's no truth, though, in the rumour that any country choosing to go with English is obliged by European Broadcasting Union rules to include the words 'destiny', 'fantasy', 'shine', 'eyes' and 'dream' in their song, with bonus points available for squeezing them all into the same sentence (which a few seem to have tried to do) plus a shout of "house!" from the EBU's Voting Scrutineer.

Nevertheless, some of the decisions regarding what language to go with have been somewhat bold (i.e. 'odd' if you're being generous, 'inexplicable' if you're not). Cyprus (official languages Greek and Turkish, and part of the British Commonwealth) in 2007 and Austria (official language German) in 2016 both went with French, for instance. Other countries have adopted a kind of reverse psychology approach and embraced obscurity full on, with arguably predictable results in terms of scoreboard success. Norway in 1980 famously let their anti-hydropower protest song embrace little-known Sami, for example, while the 2004 Estonian entry 'Tii' ('Road') was delivered entirely in the Võro tongue spoken (that bloke in that pub once told me) by less than a hundred thousand people in the south-eastern part of the country.

But in terms of leftfield language selection, there's another option too – and an engagingly perverse one as well. I'm not that well up on precisely how many different languages are spoken in Eurovision countries so I asked my informant at the pub and he said "lots". So let's take that as official. Why, then, when you're penning your Eurovision classic, would you give them all the bum's rush and decide to invent one of your own just for the occasion? It's like those Star Trek fans who actually devised a language called Klingon. Now there's an idea for Eurovision.

I've already mentioned Belgium's near miss in 2003. To misquote someone famous, to fail to win Eurovision with an artificial language on one occasion might be viewed as a misfortune; to do it twice just looks a bit daft. Yet that's exactly what happened when Ishtar turned up with 'O Julissi' in 2008, again with those arguably predictable results. Not that this should be regarded as a purely

112

Belgian phenomenon. Evidence actually suggests it may be a slightly broader Low Countries thing, as two years previously Dutch all-girl trio Treble had headed for Athens armed with 'Amambanda'. Now (I think) Treble were trying to convey the point that language need not be an insurmountable barrier by framing much of their song in an imaginary tongue; paradoxically, however, by framing much of their song in an imaginary tongue and failing to secure very much in the way of non-imaginary votes, they actually proved that language may indeed be an insurmountable barrier. I think I like that.

Perhaps, judging from their energetic, extensively bongo-based performance, the Treble girls genuinely believed all future international co-operation and collaboration could be underpinned by a shared appreciation of *djembe* drums. And they may even be right. But their visionary message sadly passed way over the heads of the Eurovision voting public, who (judging from the results of that 2006 Semi-Final) vastly preferred songs about sexually predatory women and hard rock to a tune extolling common humanity and sketching out a tantalising vision of world peace. Come on, now. Hand on heart, can you say you're even the tiniest, tiniest bit surprised?

3. 'Kitchen Sink' Songs

Less is more, they say. Not in my book. For me, 'less' is rarely enough and it certainly doesn't get my vote over 'far, far too much'. At Eurovision, stripped-back does have its place, of course, and I'm not just talking about those Bucks Fizz-style tear-off-clothes moments that have evolved into one of the contest's most enduring trademarks. But as a general rule of thumb, when it's a Eurovision title that's up for grabs, you can never have an excess of excess. If you're in two minds about something, do it anyway. If a solitary violinist's just not enough, add an ice skater. If your song needs just a little bit more bounce in it, go get yourself a trampoline.

113

Naturally, I reserve special affection for those entries that simply don't know when to stop, that keep throwing more and more elements into the mix in a desperate 'no regrets' strategy that can only end in a breathless, beautiful, chaotic maelstrom which leaves the viewer – caught in a kind of multi-sensory crossfire – mildly traumatised.

I could flag up any number of examples for you. I could, for instance, direct your attention to the Czech entry in 2008 – a very nice little pop song called 'Have Some Fun'. But having a very nice little pop song clearly wasn't enough. When it came to the Semi-Final, it found itself submerged like a fragile Russian doll beneath myriad layers of noise, din and fury centring on a bellowing DJ and his double record deck, pillars of flame, club beats, dry ice, multiple additional synthesisers, intrusive 'tishing' hi-hat, sparkling fireworks, two hyperactive foil-clad dancers plus panning, dipping, swirling camera shots that seemed to have been taken by a stealth fighter on a low-level strafing mission. For plucky singer Tereza Kerndlová, trying to deliver the simple melody with all that going on must have been like having three darts to hit double top on the deck of a fishing boat pitching in a force eight North Sea gale – and with a bellowing trawlerman shouting down her ear as she took aim. By the end of the song (which didn't qualify for the Grand Final) I was suffering from a touch of motion sickness and had the first signs of a pressure headache coming on. Magnificent stuff!

But my absolute favourite 'kitchen sink' song – and still a firm fixture in my all-time Eurovision Top Twenty – was a 2009 classic from Ukraine. This quirky masterpiece, 'Be My Valentine! (Anti-Crisis Girl)', was another hyperactive gem conceived and delivered by one of the queens of Ukrainian pop, the uncompromisingly offbeat Svetlana Loboda. The song may only have lasted the regulation three minutes but packed into it was a good hour and a half's worth of world-class entertainment, in the following sequence:

114

...song starts; trio of male dancers clad as silvery Ancient Greek soldiers start raunchy moves; Svetlana pole dances with ladder; smoke discharges; tubular bells, searchlights and giant pumping graphics kick in; dancer jumps six feet onto floor from top of Svetlana's 'Hell Machine'; dancers lift Svetlana horizontal at head height while she sings second verse; more smoke discharges; dancers spin Svetlana in three hundred and sixty degree cartwheel; tubular bells, searchlights and giant pumping graphics kick in again; dancer makes obscene arm-pump gesture in audience's direction; Svetlana does aided three hundred and sixty degree backward flip; dancer does unaided three hundred and sixty degree backward flip; Svetlana finds drum kit; Svetlana sits down at drum kit and picks up drumsticks; Svetlana batters drum kit; Svetlana sticks tongue out; dancers use guy-ropes to man-haul drum kit to centre of stage with Svetlana still battering it; Svetlana throws away drumsticks; tubular bells, searchlights and giant pumping graphics kick in again; Svetlana stands on drum kit; wind machine fires up; two Ukrainian flags ripple majestically in the wind; Svetlana and dancers gyrate towards song's cacophonous conclusion; kitchen sink falls from ceiling and lands in front of Svetlana...

OK, that last bit didn't happen. But the greatest possible compliment I can pay Svetlana's startling shock-and-awe entry is that it didn't even have to.

2. Shouty Blokes

Some of Mother Nature's most wondrous sights are also the very rarest. Volcanic lighting, bioluminescence and lenticular clouds, for example. Or a gas fitter who's got all the correct tools and all the right-sized spare parts with them. So it is at Eurovision. Specifically, so it is with shouty blokes. We're talking very occasional, very scarce sightings here – but for that very reason they're especially worth savouring and sticking in your mental Eurovision Hall of Fame.

Of course, shouting isn't a uniquely male phenomenon. Not in our house anyway. But in Eurovision, if there's someone behind the lead singer who's being a bit shouty, it's almost certainly going to be a man. And what a strange and remarkably entertaining sight it makes, as well, though I can't remotely explain why. I've already mentioned the Czech DJ from 2008, who peppered 'Have Some Fun' (and the back of Tereza Kerndlová's head) with all manner of random yells, yelps, hollers and howls for no apparent or particularly pressing reason. Absolutely brilliant stuff.

But easily my favourite instance – a display of top-quality shouty singing – graces another fixture in my all-time Eurovision Top Twenty: the joyous 'Love Song' by Poland's Blue Café, which lit up the Grand Final in 2004 in an excellent, shouty way. My two favourite aspects of this textbook example, beautifully delivered by the band's guitarist, are (i) his perfectly executed slow shouty walk from the back of the stage up to his microphone stand at the very start of the song, and (ii) his faultless shouty bloke microphone technique, keeping the mike well away from his mouth to minimise possible distortion and to maximise shouty impact. And there are still another couple of world-class shouty interventions to enjoy as the song gallops in lithe Latino style towards its punch-punch, punch-punch-punch conclusion. It's a true Eurovision shouty classic – and never forget that a true Eurovision shouty classic really is a thing of rare and shouty beauty.

1. Hats

Now here's a topic. I'll bet – or perhaps I just hope – that someone, somewhere has written a PhD thesis on 'The Social, Cultural and Political Significance of Hat Wearing'. As an art form, successfully wearing a hat is right up there with all the big ones: sculpture, lithography, choral singing, ceramics, experimental dance and arranging a cutlery drawer so it looks just right. But for my money, where headwear's the issue, you're always walking a tightrope.

There's a very fine line indeed between appearing extremely dapper, cool or rakish and making yourself look like a complete tool. Context is a key part of the problem, of course. If you're showing a prospective purchaser around your house, for example, think very carefully about whether that Napoleon-style bicorne is really going to create the right mood for a sale.

Given how finely balanced such matters of taste are, it's not surprising that Eurovision has seen a veritable cascade of THMs (Terrible Hat Misjudgements) down through the decades. Usually, these stem from a complete lack of self-awareness on the performer's part – a fatal absence of understanding that, while they may very well think wearing that particular hat at that particular jaunty angle makes them look like a bit of a dude, the viewing public may not share that analysis. In any walk of life, wearing any sort of hat is a pretty brave decision and at Eurovision in particular, with its multiplicity of cultures, traditions and ethno-geographic perceptions about what makes a man look like a right royal knob, we really do start entering *légion d'honneur* territory.

This is, then, archetypal eye of the beholder stuff – especially when the beholding hat-wearer (male or female) is admiring themselves in the mirror just prior to heading out on the Eurovision stage. Is it a case of "yes...looking so good!" or is it an "mmm...maybe not..."? You'll just have to reach your own verdict, for instance, on the fearsome sextet of Latvian top hats paraded by Bonaparti.lv in the 2007 contest, or the trendy burgundy trilby sported by the splendid Serhat for San Marino in the first Semi-Final in 2016. Of course, any name that actually includes the word 'hat' should give us a pretty clear picture of the direction of travel and, from my viewpoint, certainly ticks the hat box.

And there's no room for any debate whatsoever about the simply magnificent three-foot furry black pointy 'winkle-pickers' worn so spectacularly by Moldovan hardcore/folklore ethno-rockers Zdob şi

Zdub in 2011 – headwear nicely counterpointed by the three-foot furry white pointy 'winkle-picker' worn by their horn-blowing unicyclist (that's right, a horn-blowing unicyclist) in what was actually also a very accomplished bid for Eurovision 'kitchen sink' status.

Given the many perils involved in headwear selection, it's all the more reason to salute those Eurovision acts who really know how to pull off a hat, so to speak. Indeed, sometimes that's quite literally the case. As Stefan Raab and his band demonstrated for Germany in 2000, when they flung off their stetsons so unceremoniously a mere thirty seconds into 'Wadde Hadde Dudde Da?', sometimes the act of hat removal reveals an intriguing ambiguity towards the act of hat wearing. Perhaps even, I'd like to think, a profound understanding of the cultural relativism involved in the whole process. (I'll concede that I may have been over-thinking this hat thing.) Not forgetting, of course, that in 2016 Serhat generously propelled his own hat into the crowd right at the end of 'I Didn't Know'. Arise, Sir Hat, indeed.

But my ultimate Eurovision Hat Hero just has to be Gökhan Özoğuz, lead singer with Turkish ska punk band Athena, who achieved an excellent fourth-placed finish with the high-octane, crowd-stoking 'For Real' in Istanbul in 2004. As the band get busy laying down a brass-fuelled platform of upbeats, offbeats and chopbeats, Gökhan prowls onto the stage, slightly crouched, in tartan-style trousers and black trilby-style hat. And as he stops, bows and casts a look of detached amusement towards the crowd, he plucks the hat clean off his head with a casual wristy flourish and nonchalantly flings it Frisbee-style far away to his right. "I'll be the one who decides where, when and for how long wearing a Eurovision hat may or may not be appropriate," he seems to be saying. At least to me, anyway. But, as I say, maybe I've been over-thinking this whole hat business. OK, I'll stop thinking about it now. Completely. I won't dwell on it anymore. I'll put it right out of my mind. That's it. Gone. I really won't be thinking about Gökhan Özoğuz's Eurovision hat ever again. Gone completely.

I wonder if anyone caught it?

Postcard: Saturday 19th April 1980

Let me talk to you now about something that I'm sure preys on your mind quite a bit: set design. Over the last decade or so, Eurovision stages have really ramped up in terms of what can be achieved in delivering a big 'hey wow'. But despite the relentless march of progress – and, specifically, the march of clever things that go flicker, flash and fizz – my all-time favourite Eurovision set is still the one that graced Malmö in 1992, as Sweden hosted the contest for the third time and seized the chance to remind everyone just how scary and hairy their ancestors had been. The vast Viking longship prow that dominated the stage didn't just dwarf the performers. From the front-on camera angle, it looked like it was actually about to mow them down – with the exception of the hyper-hirsute Danish singer, who looked like he'd probably just climbed out of it.

I particularly remember the 1992 contest as this was the one where I first road-tested a Eurovision Night phrase that's really stood the test of time for me ever since. Please feel free to use it yourself, assuming you don't already. I'd like to think it'll mark you out among your fellow revellers as a bit of a Eurovision sage and an individual of surprising depth and insight. It'll also get you and your reputation out of a huge hole if you've spent the run-up to the contest banging on about song X or song Y and how it just can't fail to win – only to see its chances sabotaged on the night by an off-key falsetto ambush, a creepy wink to camera or the presence of an inadvisable violin. Just slowly shake your head from side to side, more in disappointment than in anger, and mutter knowingly: "it's just not translating well to the stage..." And if you REALLY want to set your stall out as one of Eurovision's in-crowd, you can even streamline this to the pithier: "no – it's just not translating..."

In all truth, I could have done with this phrase a few years earlier when Eurovision entered a bit of a doldrums in the second half of the 1980s and sometimes whole contests would pass by where I'd struggle to find a single song whose mast I could nail my colours to. But that certainly hadn't been an issue right at the start of the decade, when I often found myself submerged by an embarrassment of riches as I tried to pinpoint my favourite song of the night. Sometimes, the thought would even cross my mind that it might have been better if they hadn't chucked so many classics at me in one go. But as the old saying goes, be careful what you wish for – a phrase that often pops into my head whenever I think of the cleavage-heavy, laundry-scrubbing, butter-churning 2014 Polish entry 'My Słowianie – We Are Slavic'.

Where was I? Oh yes. While scarcely infallible, the Swedes certainly know a bit about visual impact at Eurovision. They know about longship prows and they know about little animated people carried away by animated balloons. They know about star guitars and golden shoes. Above all, they know all about the simple yet deadly effectiveness of the leather 'n' leopard-skin look so effortlessly carried off by their representative at the 1980 contest in The Hague – a contest which to this very day remains my all-time favourite Eurovision. Yes, in much the same way as some people tend to look back and think "those were MY Olympics", "that was MY World Cup" or "they were MY European Extreme Ironing Championships', so 1980 was MY Eurovision. In fact, I feel I could watch it all over again, right now. Or as they say in Sweden, *just nu*...

*   *   *   *   *   *

We're in the Netherlands because, having chalked up the second of their back-to-back wins with 'Hallelujah' in Jerusalem twelve and a half months ago, Israel have decided they can't afford to stage two Eurovisions in a row. Nor are they actually present this year to go for an unprecedented hat-trick of victories as some brainbox has decided to stage the contest on a Jewish holy day. It's a bit like someone hosting a birthday party for you and then not actually inviting you to it – or holding it on a night when they know for an absolute fact you've got tickets for a Racey concert. Talk about diary clashes. But tragically we're still a few years away from the Filofax explosion so it's simply not physically possible for anyone to organise anything properly yet.

But we're in pretty safe hands in The Hague for this, Eurovision's twenty-fifth edition. Once Charpentier has done his party piece (can't he write something new?), we're treated to a quick shot of a lone fiddler shuffling along a North Sea beach and then a selection box of Dutchified scenes before being whisked into the Congresgebouw to meet conductor Rogier van Otterloo and the Metropole Orchestra. Actually, his name's already familiar to me from a '70s solo album by Thijs van Leer, master flute-touting multi-instrumentalist with Dutch prog-rock pioneers Focus. And appropriately, the introductory music specially composed by Rogier for tonight's show could pass as an obscure Focus b-side, with just a sprinkling of Van der Valk chucked in for a little added Dutchification.

As if any's needed. Even the microphone held by our charming host Marlous Fluitsma, who's resplendent in sparkling pink, looks a bit like a tulip. And fertile ground seems to be a subliminal theme tonight, with Eurovision innovations abounding. Morocco's involvement brings Africa into the fold for the very first time, while guest announcers from each country have been airlifted in to introduce their respective entries – a nicely inclusive touch certain to drag the evening out just a bit longer than absolutely necessary.

First of our nineteen contenders is Austria. Five-piece vocal group Blue Danube are giving us 'Du Bist Musik' ('You Are Music'), which quickly descends into a game of great composer bingo as the boys and girls reel off a long list of names from Mahler and Mozart to Puccini and Rossini, but skipping over Racey. I must have missed the line where they name-checked Focus but there's a nice bit of

Manfred Mann-style synth in there just to prog-rock it all up a little anyway, even though acid lagoons and Odin's loins don't get much of a look-in. Next.

Of all the adjectives available, it's not often you'd describe a Eurovision entry as uncompromising. But Turkey's song 'Pet'r Oil' is, as its title strongly suggests, uncompromisingly all about petrol. Maybe it'll summarise state-of-the-art oil exploration and extraction techniques, reference the spot price for Brent crude or reel off a list of fuel ratings for top-selling family saloon cars. My scepticism, however, proves to be entirely misplaced. Delivered with huge aplomb by Ajda Pekkan in a rippling light blue dress, THIS MAY ACTUALLY BE THE BEST SONG EVER. It's certainly the best song I've ever heard about petrol. And that includes Elvis Costello's 'Pump It Up', which probably doesn't count anyway. With its eastern rhythms and evocative instrumentation conjuring up visions of jasmine groves, camel trains and naughty nights at the caravanserai, this is Turkey's best entry to date by a massive margin.

Well, there's a thing. No sooner have the Turks taken the trouble to extract the oil and hydrocrack it into petrol than the Greeks want to burn it all up again. 'Autostop' is a quirky, perky but slightly odd ode to the pleasures of hitchhiking. That's right, hitchhiking. And is it International List Day or something? Picking up the baton from the Austrians, Anna Vissi and her compatriots rattle off a catalogue of places you could conceivably hitchhike to or from, leaving me to wonder whether it's too late to insert a list of FA Cup winners into the UK entry. Oh and here are the first la-la-la's of the evening, impeccably delivered by Anna and chums who are dressed in black rounded off by stylish red presumably in recognition of the colour you're most often confronted with when you're staring at traffic lights in downtown Athens on a Monday morning.

Problem. I'm enjoying the show but I'm a little concerned regarding the lack of songs about penguins. But right on cue to save the day here's Luxembourg to tell us all about 'Papa Pingouin'. This awesome responsibility rests with Sophie & Magaly who take to the stage looking like the Toyah Twins clad in matching pink and blue boiler suits, so they'll be more than capable of lending a hand if the Greeks' car breaks down or runs out of the Turks' petrol. And oh, here's a man in a penguin outfit. And oops, he's lost his footing as he waddles up the step. But quell that cynicism! AND FORGET EVERYTHING I SAID ABOUT THE TURKISH ENTRY BECAUSE THIS IS THE BEST SONG EVER! It's simplistic in a nursery rhyme way, but it's got a hook to die for. Catchy doesn't even begin to describe a song that appears to be about a penguin going on holiday. And what on earth's the matter with that, as long as it's got the requisite travel insurance and booked the time off with its employer in advance?

Oh – here's the inevitable list, this time of perfect penguin holiday destinations. Apparently, these include Paris, Rome and (strangely) Carthage, which I thought the Romans had razed to the ground. They must have left the holiday village intact. Meanwhile, penguin man just about makes it down the step before showing off his bum unnecessarily (I didn't realise it was that kind of holiday) and indulging in a quick penguin pogo. But don't let any of that detract from what we've just witnessed. If I'd written a hook like that, I'd be high-fiving complete strangers in Starbucks for a fortnight.

Now here's that bit of history I promised you as Morocco arrive with the contest's first-ever song from Africa and also its first-ever song in Arabic. It's called 'Bitakat Hob' ('Song for Peace') and apparently Samira Bensaïd started singing at nine so she must be getting tired as it's gone half-past eight. I reckon it needs more penguins – the song, I mean, not Morocco. But it's all very creditable and very pleasant and it sets us up for the Italian entry. Right. Let me try to say something positive. Well, his hair looks like it's in exemplary condition. And there's a nice falsetto ambush when the chorus arrives but, to be honest, there's only so much a cracking pair of purple trousers can do in the battle for hearts and minds.

On to Denmark, represented by a bunch of guys from Aarhus (in the middle of our street, presumably). They're all dressed in dungarees as if they've just broken off from a bit of Artexing and frankly (no offence) I've had a more entertaining three minutes reading the Dulux colour chart. Nothing's really happening and the backing singers look a bit awkward – probably keen to nip down the DIY store to pick up some more rawlplugs. Sorry but you'd be pretty disappointed to finish below this one on the scoreboard. Let's call it tonight's 'minimum requirement' entry. An entry-level entry, if you like.

Who's up next? Ah, yes – Sweden. With a song called 'Just Nu'. And FORGET EVERYTHING I SAID ABOUT THE TURKISH AND LUXEMBOURG ENTRIES BECAUSE THIS IS ACTUALLY THE BEST SONG EVER! If it looks like a pop star and walks like a pop star – and kicks away the mike stand and brandishes it like Rod Stewart – IT'S A POP STAR! Leather jacket, white leopard-skin top and tight leather trousers leave nothing to chance as Tomas Ledin patrols the stage while guitars chug and quickly escort us into life-affirming chant-along chorus territory. To be honest, I'm slightly worried about the tightness of those trousers and – oh, something's fallen off. Not off Tomas or his trousers, fortunately, but off the microphone. Tomas defies trouser tightness to swoop down and sweep it up before executing an emergency refit in a matter of seconds, so he won't be needing to blag any insulating tape off our DIY Danes. Even more important is the fact that Tomas completes his running repairs in good time to lean nonchalantly on the electric piano during the second verse.

This is turning out to be a bit of a rock masterclass from Mr Ledin. Can't quite put my finger on it, though, but there's still just one thing missing. What is it? Yes, that! A big leg kick during the chorus! And the leather trousers held! Tomas struts and prowls again and then commits to another kick during the final chorus, the trousers successfully take the strain again and arguably my life is complete. Only now do I fully comprehend how rare a gift it is to be capable of combining classic rock moves with a very firm grasp of the basic principles of microphone repair and maintenance.

Then, just when you start wondering where the night's next list is coming from, up pops Switzerland's Paola with a roll call of silent movie greats as part of her pretty decent mid-paced effort 'Cinéma'. She sells it really well, in fact, and the thought crosses my mind that they could do with her as an usher down at my multiplex. I'm sure they'd shift a bit more of that odd stem-ginger ice cream that they sell now. Paola then makes way for Finland's Vesa-Matti Loiri and his song 'Huilumies' ('Flute Man'), which I'd like to think is some sort of homage to Thijs van Leer but almost certainly is nothing of the kind. Vesa-Matti holds up his flute as if to say "here's what a flute looks like". OK, got that bit. Now he puts it to his lips as if to say "here's what a flute sounds like". This really is extremely useful. It's not the most technically demanding of flute melodies but it certainly gives us an idea of the sort of thing a flute might be capable of in the right hands. Really very helpful.

OK. To help us digest all of that for a moment, I think we need a bit of a time-out. So here's Norway to slow things down a little with an unassuming acoustic ballad. Apparently it's a protest song. I'd have thought this would be the perfect moment to start a petition about the failure to regulate the number of lists creeping into Eurovision, but clearly that's not deemed as important as the proposed construction of a hydroelectric plant up there in Sami country. And what's this? A man in traditional dress ambles on to the stage to drive the point right home. Now don't get me wrong. Anyone who lives in and around the Arctic Circle semi-nomadically and successfully ekes out a living from herding reindeer has my undiluted respect and is absolutely guaranteed my undivided attention. But before we get round to tackling the hydro thing, could someone do something about all these bloody lists?

Right, we're on to Germany now. This is Katja Ebstein's third tilt at the title and this time round her dreams are riding on a very tidy little song called 'Theater', which is another place where sales of stem-ginger ice cream are possibly a little sluggish. First we see a piano keyboard plonked by hands in white fingerless gloves with small dolls sown onto the backs. I'd been wondering where I left those. And then we're into the song, which expertly plots a course through 'Cabaret' territory as Katja and her four backing-singers-cum-mime-artists prove as well-drilled as the walls those DIY Danes have presumably been working on.

Did I miss the UK entry? One moment Noel Edmonds is doing the introduction and the next Prima Donna are hanging on to the last note of 'Love Enough for Two'. I think I may have zoned out – probably something to do with that caravanserai. How did Prima Donna do? Which FA Cup winners did they mention? Will they repeat Brotherhood of Man's victory here four years ago? If I can't remember anything about the song, that's perhaps going to be a slightly tall order.

Pimp my lapels! Now it's Portuguese singer José Cid with a list of words for goodbye, a list of words for love, some cool shades and some eye-catching silvery folded flaps on the front of his jacket which help to hurl him through the bright, breezy 'Um Grande, Grande Amor' ('A Great, Great Love'). The crowd come in too early with their applause and it's unclear whether they're showing excessive appreciation or just trying to get José to stop as soon as possible. Whatever the case, he doesn't take the hint and sends the chorus round again, and when the audience have another crack at the applause thing it does indeed seem that they're all having a jolly nice time after all.

In point of fact, maybe they're just rousing themselves in readiness for the home entry, which is basically the 1974 Dutch entry but with less mouth. Quite literally, in fact, as Maggie MacNeal is flying solo here with a real crowd-pleaser. The absence of Mouth certainly isn't noticed as 'Amsterdam' blends some nice piano ripples in the verses with an oompah/street-organ-style singalong chorus and suddenly I'm overpowered with a feverish need to go and buy a plastic windmill in a nick-nack shop. The song lacks a killer big finish, though, and that might ultimately scupper its chances. But I'd say it's certainly more of a contender than the French song which, while jolly enough, has as its centrepiece some slightly odd pigeon-type cooing that makes me want to check the back of my jacket.

Just three countries left now. And here's a young chap called Johnny Logan to fly the Irish tricolour. I wonder if he's cut out for this Eurovision lark? He can certainly find his way around the sax-heavy ballad 'What's Another Year?' without any difficulty. In fact, Johnny's so wrapped up in it he looks genuinely upset, concerned and a bit distant – like he's just remembered he might have left the gas on. The last, high note is nailed and, though not my bag, this song could be a contender. I wouldn't extend that designation to the Spanish entry, though, which revolves around a 'sleep with me' plea sung by a band of Basques who are definitely heading for one exit.

Where's the evening gone? It'll soon be time for Anna Vissi to hitchhike home but first, to wrap things up, we've got Belgian electro-pop trio Telex, who've fairly recently struck chart success in the UK with their clever cover of Bill Haley's 'Rock Around the Clock'. Tonight, though, they're offering us a homage to Eurovision itself in the shape of a song economically entitled 'Euro-Vision' and FORGET WHAT I SAID ABOUT THE TURKISH, LUXEMBOURG AND SWEDISH ENTRIES BECAUSE THIS TIME, THIS REALLY IS ACTUALLY THE <u>BEST SONG EVER</u>! The band have come armed with two keyboards and something with dials on it, and they've dressed in dark jackets and white scarfs to deliver something catchy and perfect that's locked round a simple synthetic backbeat, with a funny hand-turny move accentuating the word 'Euro-Vision' during the chorus.

And as the singer gets a camera out right at the end to take a photo of the audience (who's watching who here?) – well, I'm not one to indulge in hyperbole but you can stop music right now! ALL music. For ALL time. This can never be bettered. A perfect song about a perfect thing. This is what all those composers Blue Danube were singing about strived for all those years. But they never got there, did they? No, Ludwig. No, Wolfgang Amadeus. No, Johann Sebastian! It took three unlikely-looking Belgians to insert the final full stop at the end of the book that's called the History of All Music. They even included a little electronic version of Charpentier's Eurovision theme to underline the point that perfection has now officially been achieved. The future has arrived and it's Telex who've just had the very, very, very final say. God, I need a trifle.

*   *   *   *   *   *

Well, the message that there can be no more music, ever, clearly hasn't filtered through to the Dutch Rhythm Steel and Show Band, who are providing a spot of decent cabaret before we're left at the mercy of nineteen juries consisting of eleven people, who hopefully aren't as tone-deaf as their predecessors that handed out an epic travesty to Germany's Dschinghis Khan last year in Jerusalem. Actually, the interval act's quite fun. There's obviously something about a samba beat as I now desperately want to blow a whistle or hit a cowbell (neither of which I've done for a fair number of years), while the producers periodically cut to the traditionally and entertainingly slightly awkward interviews in the green room. Johnny Logan opines that there are eighteen good songs out there, which begs the question – which one is Johnny leaving out?

Marlous has a white phone in front of her and I wonder if the banker will be dialling in for a quick word with Noel Edmonds. Indeed, the voting sequence will see Marlous effortlessly flit between all manner of phone designs and even wheel out an outsized walkie-talkie to make contact with Helsinki, despite the risk of having someone's eye out with the aerial. First up, though, it's a very distant-sounding Austria who initially appear to be speaking through a wormhole as they thoughtfully donate their first point to Luxembourg's penguin before lobbing eight at Germany, ten at Ireland and twelve at the Dutch. They also give Belgium nothing at all, clearly recognising that you just can't demean an entry of that calibre with something as mundane or as grubby as 'points'. The Turkish spokesperson also seems to have been sucked into the same wormhole as Austria and, fair play, it must be very hard to read out marks with five G-force bearing down on your face. Twelve more to the Dutch.

The Greek spokesperson, by contrast, sounds like they're locked somewhere near the Earth's core dodging the magma flows, but three points for Belgium hint briefly at an appreciation of genius before they actually try to award marks to The Hague. Crikey, if you're going to start awarding marks to individual cities, we'll be here all weekend! And as more juries declare, Germany, Ireland, the Netherlands and, briefly, Sweden all perform strongly before a burst of support for the UK brings them into contention too.

But as the time comes for the Norwegian jury to declare and Marlous now grabs hold of a big red phone – presumably the hotline she's been using to keep Queen Juliana of the Netherlands in touch with developments – not only are Belgium rooted to last place; daylight is now appearing between Ireland and the rest. It's not all cut and dried and Germany could still snatch it, until the very last jury award the seven points for the Germans that leaves them short of the Irish and a ten for Ireland puts the lid on it.

Though Belgium have hauled themselves up to the dizzy heights of seventeenth place, the focus is on those at the other end of the scoreboard as Johnny Logan and Katja Ebstein hug in the green room, Johnny does a quick pogo and presumably reflects on whether he should take some sort of list with him when he heads back out on stage. In a nice touch, the trophy is presented by Marcel Bezençon, who first came up with the idea for the Eurovision Song Contest a quarter of a century ago. The writer of 'What's Another Year?' pops on a black boater, Johnny blows a kiss to someone in the crowd, tonight's remaining contestants drift on stage and the Norwegian singers, I'd like to think, wander round trying to get anyone who's interested to sign their petition.

Meanwhile, forlorn and disconsolate, I'm left to consider starting up a petition of my own. Justice for Belgium. And Sweden while I'm at it.

Travesty Totality

As medieval warlords go, it's fair to say that Genghis Khan has had some pretty mixed reviews. There's no doubting his military accomplishments, singleness of purpose or success in founding history's largest contiguous empire. But some of his methods probably wouldn't have won him a Man of the Year award at Amnesty International's annual conference. Whichever way you look at it, though, there's one gaping hole in his CV: he never had a Eurovision winning song named after him. And while the likes of Tamerlane and Osman Bey also have a frustrating gap against their names in that same column, they've never come remotely as close as Genghis.

Indeed, if there were any justice in our unjust world, he'd long ago have joined Napoleon in what's actually a pretty short list of autocrats explicitly name-checked in victorious Eurovision entries. Because when Germany's Dschinghis Khan turned up in Jerusalem in 1979 to sing their song 'Dschinghis Khan' about Dschinghis (or Genghis) Khan, it was as plain as the nose on your face (which the man himself may very well have cut off for you) that this masterpiece was going to carry all before it. But it didn't. It didn't even come second. Or third. Even a performance on the night of magisterial colour and zest – with the group admittedly dressed more like extras from Doctor Who during the Tom Baker years than nomadic thirteenth-century warriors – wasn't able to drag it into the top three, let alone to the top of the shop.

I simply couldn't get my head around it. But I can now. Because it finally dawned on me some years later that the Eurovision Song Contest is not one but two events. First, you get to watch a load of songs. Second, you get to watch a load of voting. These two events may be connected in some way. But then again, maybe they won't. So in 1979, 'Dschinghis Khan' clearly won the first bit. But it clearly didn't win the second bit, because Gali Atari and Milk & Honey did with 'Hallelujah'. Two events, you see.

It's vital to make this distinction. Otherwise, it can really eat you up. You tune in year after year to see your favourite entries fed into the Eurovision mincing machine, chewed up, spat out and finishing seventeenth. Or worse. You'll then be consumed by the burning feeling that something terrible has happened, that justice is once again asleep at the wheel and that the guilty men and women (be they jury members or televoters) will never, ever be held accountable for their sins in an International Court of Eurovision Travesties. Even writing a letter of complaint to your Euro MP will almost certainly prove to be the most futile of futile gestures. All you can do to vent the pain is make a badge saying 'I've Been Travestied' and flaunt it before an uncaring world, or set up some sort of floral tribute in your garden and tend it assiduously until the petals fall, the leaves curl and, finally, new hope starts to bud and blossom again the following spring.

But then, eventually, it dawns on you. Those acts of larceny, those heists, those hold-ups, those shameful acts of daylight night-time robbery that see palpably lesser songs snatch the Eurovision crown at the expense of obviously superior specimens – well, they're actually a key ingredient of the Eurovision Song Contest. Without them, your whole Eurovision experience would somehow be diminished. And the bigger the travesty, the better. Only when the sunlight of sense and reason is comprehensively obscured in a kind of Eurovision eclipse in which complete totality is achieved and the entire world of music seems submerged in utter darkness, does the real significance of yet another Eurovision travesty become fully clear. Only now will you get that surge of anger and disorientation that says you know better than the world and that – in a kind of Eurovision Freemasonry kind of way – only you have access to secret truths, arcane knowledge and musical mysteries simply beyond the comprehension of lesser mortals. And that's when you get to comfort yourself with the thought that a lot more people in the world read Dan Brown than Fyodor Dostoyevsky. And in the 1980s a lot more people listened to Stars on 45 than to Telex.

So let's toast the travesties. Let's embrace the grieving process. Let's welcome the fact that a travesty-free Eurovision wouldn't be a recognisable Eurovision at all and we'd have to look elsewhere for unimpeachable forensic proof that other people are much more stupid than we are, that we're the only visionaries left on the planet and that even 'the experts' know a hell of a lot less about the really important things in life than we do.

*   *   *   *   *   *

Julius Caesar – yet another autocrat who's so far strangely slipped the net where Eurovision winners are concerned – once famously wrote that Gaul was divided into three parts. If he'd been writing about travesties of justice at the Eurovision Song Contest, however, he'd no doubt have explained that these can be split up into five distinct categories. And then he'd have gone and set fire to a couple of Gallic villages. He was a bit like that, I'm afraid.

So as he's just a little busy at the moment, allow me to guide you through a taxonomy of travesty types that almost certainly isn't exhaustive. But hopefully it can serve the purpose of demonstrating how there's hidden order in all things and that a kind of divine geometry lurks behind even the most outrageous stitch-ups routinely doled out to the undeserving by the mischievous gods of Eurovision.

1.   The 'Inverted Scoreboard' Travesty

Does anyone ever actually rub their eyes in disbelief? I'm not sure they do. But there literally are metaphorical times when you metaphorically literally rub your eyes in disbelief as you're confronted by the final scoreboard at the end of Eurovision Night. You say to yourself, I understand my favourite song might not have been everyone's cup of tea. I appreciate that he, she or they looked a bit odd, creepy or ripe for arrest. I know it was a pretty bad call to include that granny-vote-deterring slut-dance option. But what's it doing right down THERE? THAT is a <u>JOKE</u>!

One point. ONE POINT! That was all Yugoslavia found their efforts rewarded with in 1991 as they staggered back to port, holed below the waterline by the torpedo of jury indifference, in twenty-first place – with just Austria preventing them from plummeting into the void of Eurovision last-place embarrassment. And right then and there, a classic Eurovision travesty 'stream of consciousness rant' started running through my mind…

Am I misinterpreting the scoreboard? Has there been a rule change so the lowest score wins? Are you seriously saying that some of that other pap deserved to finish above 'Brazil'? You absolutely cannot tell me it's not a classic Eurovision song! OK, I understand Baby Doll herself may be an acquired taste. But don't get spooked – that silver heels, light-blue tights and blond beehive look will be all the rage by August. On our estate, anyway. And you've got to admit this hook-crammed samba fest was catchier than gastro-enteritis at an all-weekend open-air pop festival. It's only two years since Yugoslavia won this damn thing and you simply CANNOT tell me 'Brazil' is twenty places worse than 'Rock Me'. NOTHING IS! And can I just point out that it went down big in the hall? As we all know, that's a far more scientific guide to the worth of any Eurovision entry than the opinions of humourless juries holed up in windowless attic rooms lit by a single thirty-watt light bulb, with just a flickering portable telly for company as they scrawl down their worthless marks on curled-up yellow stickies re-used from last year…

Since the introduction of Semi-Finals into the Eurovision process, of course, this breed of travesty has also expanded to include the 'Didn't Make It to the Grand Final' travesty. (See Chapter 13 to revisit the biggest Eurovision mass extinction event in history.) But it's always incorporated the 'Didn't Make It to Eurovision at All' travesty, which continues to see many great songs cut down like rye at harvest time at the national selection stage – songs such as Maia Vahtramäe's superb 'Üle Vesihalli Taeva' ('Above the Watery Grey Sky') whose flame was extinguished at Estonia's Eesti Laul in 2015. Similarly, in 2016, to my ears at least, Poland let a sure-fire winner slip right through their fingers as Margaret's brilliant 'Cool Me Down' somehow proved surplus to requirements. Just for the record, the result shocked me into abstaining from paprika crisps and half-wheat/half-rye bread for the entire week.

2. The 'Understandable' Travesty

Sometimes you love a Eurovision song but you know, in your heart of hearts, it's got no chance of corralling much support from those with the power to shape destinies and build or destroy careers. It's a bit like modern art. That white canvas with the yellow dot on it is certainly basic, but you kind of like it. Clearly, on the artist's part, it was thirty seconds well spent. But you totally understand why others walk straight past it and moan about it later in the café. "It was just a dot. On a canvas. A dot on a canvas! How much did they pay for that? Are you going to finish that fudge cake?"

So it is with some Eurovision entries. You love them. And don't get me wrong, it absolutely IS a travesty that other people don't share the passion, but at the same time it's kind of comprehensible why that's the case. Into this category I'd reluctantly place the 1986 Dutch entry, 'Alles Heeft Ritme' ('Everything Has Rhythm') by four-strong all-girl vocal group Frizzle Sizzle, although this mildly reggaefied, tropical fruit-juice of an offering surely could have hoped for better than thirteenth place. But probably the best dot-on-a-canvas example from my gallery of Eurovision no-hopers is the Austrian entry from 1978, 'Mrs Caroline Robinson' by three-piece band Springtime. To my ears, this was quite a clever song somewhat reminiscent of The Kinks – a mildly surreal piece about a witch with a predilection for telepathy and television, in that order. Judging from its finishing fifteenth out of twenty, though, it went straight over the heads of the juries, a bit like the song's eponymous heroine in the air balloon which was, if I understood correctly, her chosen method of transport. A veritable lost classic.

3. The 'Jaw Dropper' Travesty

It's a good job I generally watch Eurovision sitting down. Because every so often a travesty will come along that's so inexplicable, so utterly baffling and bewildering, so contrary to all the laws of nature, that only the act of sitting on a sofa can save me from spinning down a wormhole and ending up with the Austrian and Turkish juries from 1980. When these moments happen, I usually assume I'm in one of those lucid dreams where I'm actually still asleep but think I'm awake, and will only realise I'm still asleep when the door opens and in walk all the European Broadcasting Union's Eurovision Voting Scrutineers dating back to Miroslav Vilček, who'll proceed to recreate Ruslana's 'Wild Dances' on our best rug before enquiring whether there's any Port Salut that needs finishing.

Yes, these moments of high travesty are the Jaw Droppers. And Jaw Droppers may never adequately be explained, much like the disappearance of Lord Lucan or the reason why there's no 'silent' setting on your in-laws. The only really sensible response, of course, is to pretend it never happened. That's why Glennis Grace won Eurovision in 2005 for the Netherlands with 'My Impossible Dream', having walked the Semi-Final by a record margin and then romped home on the Saturday in an embarrassingly one-sided contest. That's right. No combination of Norwegian Glam Rock, Austrian yodelling or Ukrainian rap could deny our Glennis claiming the spoils which her near-faultless performance of one of Eurovision's finest power ballads so richly deserved.

So much for my parallel reality. Meanwhile, in what normal people laughingly like to refer to as 'the real world', Glennis never actually negotiated the Semi-Final's notoriously perilous path through the quicksand of travesty and never made it to the firmer terrain of artistic justice. In fact, it wasn't even a near miss as she limped in fifteenth out of twenty-five and well off the tenth place that would have provided the last passport to the Grand Final.

What made it even worse was the cruel and tortuous process whereby the ten winners from the Semi-Final were announced. This involved the marvellous Ukrainian presenters Masha and Pasha – Maria Efrosinina and Pavlo Shylko – plucking cards out of green envelopes and flashing them at the camera to reveal the names of the lucky qualifiers. Now with this kind of process, it's easy enough to keep the dread in check for the first two or three 'reveals' – and by this I mean the dread that a dire injustice is about to unfold before your very eyes. But when the fifth and sixth cards have been displayed and your favourites still haven't found the lifeboat, a feeling of terrible foreboding takes over – the sort of knot in the stomach you thought you'd said goodbye to forever when you stopped doing times-table tests at primary school. Yet still, still you cling on to that sliver of hope, that unquenchable belief that even the last envelope will see eternal justice wield her sword to good effect and set the scales of truth aright. Or failing that, the belief that the Voting Scrutineer will step in afterwards and say there's been a terrible mistake and the envelopes actually contained the names of the countries that _didn't_ qualify.

Oh yes. Straw-clutching is an essential skill for any serious Eurovision fan – and never more so than when a top-quality Jaw

Dropper threatens to shatter your childlike belief in truth, order and beauty.

4.   The 'Unfavoured Nation' Travesty

You don't get to my age thinking life's fair. In fact, I got over that idea as soon as I was first passed over for my primary school's football team. Our teacher decided that my silky skills and wide range of passing with both inside and outside of the foot would make less impact on the result of the grudge match with our arch-rivals than picking the really big bloke with anger management issues who would put himself about a bit and, by the end of the match, reduce the number of fully fit and active players the opposition would be able to field by around three-quarters. We still lost three-nil, as it happens, which only serves to underline the perils of 'pragmatic' team selection.

In the case of the Eurovision Song Contest, there's no question in my mind that some countries have to punch well above their weight to get their just desserts while others can get away with punching well below it and still end up with a decent points victory. What that means in practical terms is that some countries are far more travesty-prone than others. One example of this was provided by the perennial travails of Bulgaria, until Poli Genova's high-class 'If Love Was a Crime' secured fourth place in 2016 – a result superbly backed up, of course, by Kristian Kostov's 'Beautiful Mess' in 2017. Now you may generally have liked Bulgaria's entries before Poli turned things round last year or you may not. That's not really the point. Personally, I loved 2008's 'DJ, Take Me Away' which was, strangely enough, taken away at the Semi-Final stage. But the sight of turntables aflame was always likely to be too much for some sheltered types.

So I'll point you instead towards the run of three Bulgarian entries from 2010 to 2012. First, Miro's 'Angel Si Ti' ('You're an Angel');

then Poli Genova's 'Na Inat' ('In Spite'); then Sofi Marinova's 'Love Unlimited'. All got a Semi-Final drubbing for their troubles. All deserved much better. But whether they meet your boat-floating criteria or not, I'd suggest that there are several other countries which, had they entered these songs, would have seen all three sail into the Grand Final. I'm not going to say which countries, because they may well still have access to video footage of my daughter and I singing their Eurovision entries outside their embassies dotted around Europe – a strange holiday ritual that's passed many a drizzly afternoon in many a diplomatic quarter, I can tell you. Well, it beats looking at yellow dots on a white canvas. Since you ask, though, 'Shady Lady' outside the Ukrainian embassy in The Hague and 'Me & My Guitar' outside the Belgian embassy in Prague remain my favourite embassy Eurovision performances. Special.

5. The 'Ahead of Its Time'/'Too Good for Eurovision' Travesty

The key to being a good historian, so I'm told, is the ability to explain the 'why' rather than simply the 'what'. Personally, I'd have thought the 'where' and the 'when' were quite important too, and the 'who' wouldn't go amiss on occasions either. Still, coming up with the reason why your favourite Eurovision entries completely bomb will help you get on with your life and move on from the scene of the crime in the grisly aftermath of the contest. So it can make a lot of sense to have some ready-made labels available that you can then stick on the duds and duffers you were suckered into pinning your hopes on, before you finally pack them away in your personal Eurovision Memory Museum.

Two such labels that I've used extensively down the years and indeed the decades are the old 'it was just too far ahead of its time' appellation and its very close relative 'it was actually too good for Eurovision'. To be honest, I use one or the other of these for ninety-nine percent of my favoured entries that finish anywhere lower than fifth in the Grand Final. I'm not going to reel off a list of songs that, to my eyes and ears, have warranted either of these two descriptions. Though I have to mention Telex's 'Euro-Vision', obviously. And 'Just Nu'. And 'Papa Pingouin'. On balance, probably not 'Brazil' from 1991, though.

Whatever the case, come what might on Eurovision Night, these are the labels that are sure to leave you in full possession of the moral high ground, at peace with yourself and convinced that one day, yes one day the world will finally catch up with you and your privileged insight into what the best music is. Just like the world finally caught up with me when a version of 'Papa Pingouin' made it to the very top of the French hit parade in 2006, over a quarter of a century after it could only scramble to a scandalously low ninth place at the 1980 contest.

Ultimate vindication a generation down the line – now that truly is the sign of a really top-class Eurovision travesty.

Postcard: Thursday 18th May 2006

Four hundred and forty-five million years ago, the so-called O-S extinction event wiped out over sixty percent of the Earth's marine invertebrates. Presumably it knocked out the Bulgarian entry as well. Incredibly, though, it doesn't even rank as the number-one most devastating mass extinction that's visited our planet over the past half-billion years or so. It only comes third. What a travesty. Think of the O-S as the 'Volare' or 'Dschinghis Khan' of extinction events.

Top of the tree – a tree that must have been one of those that somehow clung on gamely in the face of basalt eruptions and shameless bloc voting – is actually the P-T event that obliterated up to ninety-six percent of all species in 'The Great Dying'. But science has a habit of reassessing these things all the time, so let me take this opportunity to make a small contribution to the debate. In my book, the evidence is clear. In any discussion about mass extinction events, it's high time to include the Semi-Final of the 2006 Eurovision Song Contest.

Yes, in Athens' Olympic Indoor Hall, a whole battalion of my favourites were brought low in their droves – songs that deserved a whole lot better than eradication by an array of competitor species. In this mass extinction, though, the agent of destruction wasn't increased volcanic activity, geomagnetic reversal, or the fact that it got a bit too hot. No, this was purely mankind's doing. And make no mistake – mankind can do an awful lot of damage with a mobile phone and a list of numbers enabling them to vote for the country of their choice as many times as they want. But not, you'll note, for the best song of the evening. And so it transpired that a body of fine and noble songs ended up on the ever-expanding bonfire of blameless televoting victims.

Yet as in any mass extinction event, some of the strong who DID survive the carnage were able to exploit the evolutionary niches that opened up invitingly in front of them. And one of them would ultimately emerge dominant – a species more monster than man, but one that proved once and for all that heavy metal music was NOT an evolutionary *cul-de-sac* and could indeed adapt to the conditions presented by the Eurovision Song Contest in the age of unbridled televoting.

Welcome to the Year of the Semi-Final Mega-Travesty. Or (as I call it) the S-F M-T mass extinction event.

*   *   *   *   *   *

In the world of sport, they say semi-finals are the worst place to lose. Presumably that doesn't apply if you go on to get hammered nine-nil in the final. But I take the point – semi-final defeat is really just another version of being stopped at the door and told you're not coming in because your name's not on the list. Far better to make it into the party, even if you end up putting your back out trying to do that strange approximation of a breakdance you haven't attempted since 1987 and then need help getting down the stairs again at the end of the evening.

So here we are in 2006. This is Eurovision's third flirtation with the 'knock-out' concept but its fifth punt at supporting straplines, which started in 2002 with 'A Modern Fairytale' in Tallinn and most recently opted for the more economical 'Awakening' in Kiev last year. This time round, it's 'Feel the Rhythm!' – although my usual pre-contest foreboding means an alternative, 'Taste the Travesty!', keeps popping into my head. But there's no time to dwell on such maudlin thoughts as a few bangs on a big drum signal that we're off and out of the traps with a very tasty little musical montage combining Greek myths with Eurovision classics.

First, we're confronted by Zeus singing 'Volare' into a lightning bolt and then Poseidon brandishes his trident as we're treated to 'L'Amor est Bleu' ('Love is Blue'), the Vicky Leandros belter that came an unjustifiably distant fourth to Sandie Shaw in 1967. So we're two songs into the montage and we've already been reminded of two epic Eurovision travesties. Great. Perhaps it's an omen. Perhaps my strapline will end up being spot-on. This is better, though: Hermes is suspended on a wire singing 'Save Your Kisses for Me' – only at Eurovision, eh? – before Athena and her singling Acropolis have a dart at 'Making Your Mind Up' and Hephaestus sets fire to his own gloves to help him burn up 'A-Ba-Ni-Bi'.

But just when I'm packing away the possibility of injustice right at the back of my mind's most inaccessible cupboard, the raw wound is ripped open again as the three hundred Spartans take to the stage to launch energetically into 'Dschinghis Khan'. Actually, to be accurate, there's only eight of them. I assume the other two hundred and ninety-two are being held back as a kind of mobile reserve in case the Persians make a move on the Grand Final. Then it's Aphrodite doing 'Diva' (naturally), Grecian vases (less naturally) doing 'Waterloo' and Amazon warrior maidens doing 'Wild Dances' (naturally, again). The routine's climax sees Mount Olympus thoroughly emptied as a veritable pantheon of gods and goddesses participate in a group rendition of last year's winner, Helena Paparizou's excellent 'My Number One', before tonight's hosts Sakis Rouvas – Greece's esteemed 'Shake It' dispenser from the 2004 contest – and Maria Menounos lead us in an uplifting and strangely moving mini-version of 'Love Shine a Light'.

I have to say I thoroughly enjoyed that! The amphitheatre-styled set looks great and I really am indecently excited. We'll be enjoying or enduring twenty-three songs tonight, all in aid of trying to squeeze a quart into a pint pot that's got quite a lot of ice in it already, as these hopefuls need to be whittled down to a paltry ten to fill the

144

available berths in the Grand Final. Then it's our first view of this evening's tourist-bait postcards which are all prefaced by women coming through louvre-style doors and walking towards the camera – similar, no doubt, to the effect you'd get if you were changing for dinner in your hotel room and a strange woman suddenly walked in from the balcony and caught you in your sports briefs. Or maybe that's just me.

Armenia's first-ever entry is a solid, up-tempo, extensively ribboned song where singer André becomes a human maypole and ends up dangling his dancers like puppets. Plenty for the behaviourologists to get their teeth into there. Then it's a Bulgarian ballad and some Slovenian disco from a lad who looks like he got caught in an updraft just before he came on stage, before Andorra opt for 'bordello chic' with an oomphy ballad called 'Sense Tu' ('Without You') that's punctuated by sundry provocative poses and just the hint of a nice game of musical chairs.

Bang! Sorry, that's nothing to do with the bordello but Belarus are here. And they're here in a flurry of power chords, cartwheels and a leapfrogging Polina Smolova who's clearly looking for the quickest possible route to the front of stage so she can heave her song 'Mum' in the general direction of right between the audience's eyes. This is pretty heavy electro-pop – the type of song Eurovision lovers generally abhor but this particular Eurovision lover loves to love. It's a barrage of noise and a blizzard of energy – spins, kicks, handstands, forward rolls. And that's just me getting into it at home. Somewhere in the heart and heat of the frenzy, Polina survives an arm-socket-wrenching flip and her dancers drive through the pain barrier towards the big-kicking big finish. There's even a hint of a stagger as the lactic acid courses through burning muscles and there's definitely the sound of panting down the mike as the camera cuts away and I wait for the next lady to come through my louvre doors at me.

Albania's amiable ethnic-tinged song provides a chance to get my breath back before Belgium's Kate Ryan ignores the fact that the lighting effects make her look like she's wearing pop socks to deliver a Europop classic in the making. 'Je t'Adore' ('I Adore You') has it all: hooks, structure and lighty-up mike stands. It's pedestrian only in the sense that this is going to walk into the Grand Final – and may well take the top prize come the weekend. Cancel that table at Pizza Hut, Kate, you'll be needed on Saturday night. Even an accidental camera shot of someone's feet and a bit of old carpet backstage can't spoil a song that's definitely a couple of rungs higher on the evolutionary tree than anything else we've seen so far.

Brian Kennedy is next up for Ireland, with the ballad 'Every Song is a Cry for Love' – and in this case, of course, a plea for votes. It's classic Irish Eurovision stuff, neatly delivered by someone I've actually heard of before. And there's the ghost of Johnny Logan right there in the final, expertly held high note. No wonder the man in the crowd with the Irish tricolour feather boa looks like he's having a smashing evening. I'm struggling to engage with the Cypriot ballad, though, before we're onto much firmer, classic Eurovision territory.

I need to say two things about Monaco's entry, 'La Coco-Dance' (which I won't bother to translate). Firstly, I really like it – let's get that out of the way up front. Secondly, why is it set in Tahiti? On a musical level, it sort of works on the level of undemanding, slightly retro, cod-tropical catchiness that's just a bit silly. Coco pop, if you will. In terms of performance, it's pitched somewhere between tired and inspired but I don't really know where. Perhaps it's a combination of the grass skirts, the throat-clearing growls and the curious effect singer Séverine Ferrer's hands seem to have on the spasming male dancer. I don't know. Some might call this dumb fun. I prefer the description weird good.

And then the thermostat goes up a few notches from steamy tropical to blatant raunch when the Former Yugoslav Republic of Macedonia arrive to have their say. 'Ninanajna' (untranslatable) is a very catchy monument to short shorts and inappropriate dancing and the dancers even turn themselves into a human chair for singer Elena Risteska right at the end, which may very well signify the next stage in the long story of human evolution.

*　　*　　*　　*　　*　　*

You know, people often say to me: "Garry, was it you who pinched my family trifle?" And I either reply "yes, but it's Eurovision" or (if I'm feeling more conciliatory) indulge in the classic lie loved by all inveterate fridge-raiders: "sorry, I didn't realise it was yours". After the argument's died down, they then might well ask me if Eurovision rappers would have more success if they mingled with the crowd a bit more. And I'll say: "only if they leave a man with green hair in charge of the stage."

This is certainly the approach taken by Poland's Ich Troje this year, who've followed up their pretty successful 2003 entry 'Keine Grenzen' ('No Borders') with 'Follow My Heart', which absolutely one hundred percent ticks my Europop box. Which isn't just a box of Coco pop, as it turns out. It's all very busy visually, with golden masks, golden masks on sticks, gold-brocaded period costumes, the world's longest gold cloak, gold tassels, golden Catherine wheels, golden epaulettes you could land an Airbus 320 on – and an absolutely cracking chorus. Curiously, as rapper Real McCoy wanders casually among the crowd, much like David Attenborough in a challenging Amazonian habitat, it looks for all the world as if natural selection has determined that the hands of every single Eurovision fan have evolved to grow a protruding appendage that looks exactly like a national flag.

Just when I feared pointless ballet may have had its day, here come Russia. Mega-mulleted Dima Bilan certainly doesn't lack for confidence – or indeed for a great song which springs to life as soon as he pushes the mike stand away and leaves it rolling on the floor while 'Never Let You Go' follows its highly entertaining course and two ballerinas set about their business. That's odd – someone's broken Rule Three of the Eurovision Song Contest and left a piano unattended in a public place. Not only that but it's sprinkled with red rose petals for reasons that aren't immediately clear. But wait – Dima's spotted the piano and he's checking it out. Indeed, he's climbing onto it and talking to the petals. That's what the pressures of stardom can do to you, I suppose.

Oh dear – I shouldn't have eaten that second family trifle. The petals are moving. And a ballerina's popped up from inside the piano. Not sure how long she's been in there but she's white as a sheet. Oh apparently that's her make-up. Nor does she emerge completely from the piano, giving her the look of a half-woman/half-piano creature that may represent another one of those evolutionary dead-ends we were talking about. And the piano only wobbles slightly as Dima leaps down from it and, hopefully, straight into the Grand Final.

I don't know about you but I'm more than ready for a disco epic. And Turkey's Sibel Tüzün definitely delivers the disco goods with 'Süper Star' (see earlier note about translation) in which her dancers provide a glimpse of an alternative evolutionary path to the human-chair and human-piano scenarios by transforming themselves into a four-person star-shaped *gestalt* entity. Nor does the pace noticeably slacken when they're replaced by Ukraine's quintet of Cossack dancers with masterly 'spotting' techniques and who light up 'Show Me Your Love' with their ludicrously acrobatic take on playground skipping. My, my, those Cossacks seem very happy. I wondered if they've ever considered a career in percussion?

But now it's Finland. And blimey, it's a good job THEY didn't start off in the audience like the Real McCoy or they might well have cleared the place. Forget those evolutionary predictions – we're about to get wiped out in a zombie apocalypse. Tonight's Semi-Final may indeed go down in the annals as an extinction event as power chords crunch and metal makes it mark at Eurovision – and metal in monster masks, at that. Lordi have an anthem for us, a 'Hard Rock Hallelujah' that has very little in common with Milk & Honey but shows us what a potential Eurovision winner could sound like after the asteroid strikes. With gruff 'n' growly vocals that make Bonnie Tyler sound like the Vienna Boys' Choir, enhanced by spark-spitting guitars and a pyrotechnic display that turns the clock back to conditions on Earth when single-cell lifeforms first sploshed around in the primordial soup, we have something here which Eurovision has never seen before. And may never see again. Until Saturday.

*　　*　　*　　*　　*　　*

We may, then, have found our top predator this evening. Only one way to recover from that. And that's with a slightly awkward green room sequence that sees our hosts lapse into mild confusion and disarray, very much in line with the traditional Eurovision template. Are we staying? Are we going? Are we going to talk to any of these Eurovision stars who someone has taken considerable trouble to line up on this big sofa? The answers, of course, are 'not sure', 'who knows?' and 'obviously not'.

The Dutch entry 'Amambanda' from girl trio Treble – though 'three girls, one guitar, nine bongos' would be a more helpful descriptor – struggles to make much of an impact. And then Lithuania treat us to one of the odder sights of the evening: six suited men standing behind mikes and claiming to be Eurovision winners, which seems a little premature but that's televoting for you. Maybe they know something. In fact, as they rip through 'We Are the Winners of Eurovision' in a performance liberally sprinkled with comic genius, the thought crosses my mind that LT United look like the weirdest small business ever.

On the far left, it looks like their bank manager has come along to keep an eye on them; beside him there's the young lad from IT; then the CEO; then the man from Marketing & Sales; then the Head of Accounts; and finally, of course, the bloke who no-one's quite sure what they do but has been there for years and runs the coffee club. It's a spoof, but a good spoof capped off by the Bank Manager having some sort of severe seizure and the bloke on the other end grabbing an inadvisable violin. But is there a hint of an uncharitable boo from the crowd as they finish? Surely there's always space for a good spoof at Eurovision?

Portugal's game but pretty tepid effort is well down the food chain, unfortunately, being undermined visually by a kind of kids-who've-been-playing-with-the-dressing-up-box feel. In fact 'Gonna Make You Dance' makes Piero's 'Celebrate' from 2004 look like quite a profound piece of work. Worse than that, it isn't actually going to make us dance, so we'd better hang on to the receipt. Sweden then send out 1991 champion Carola to do a thoroughly competent and professional job on 'Invincible', which sees a wobbly-bottom-jaw vibrato get a thorough workout.

We're down to song twenty-three. And it's ABBA. Well, OK, ABBA reincarnated. Well, OK, the spirit and the sound of ABBA partially reincarnated. Estonia's 'Through My Window' is right up there near the top of tonight's tree of life as Swedish-born singer Sandra Oxenryd channels a bit of Agnetha and she and her backing singers pay homage to ABBA's 'Voulez-Vous' era look. This song absolutely bounds along. It's beautifully delivered and it's pretty impeccable pop. Indeed, it's a fresh blast of Baltic air that's coming in through this particular window and there's not a cobweb in sight. And once Bosnia-Herzegovina have run through their very pleasant, very

150

standard Balkan ballad 'Lejla', we steel ourselves for the last song of the evening.

It's fair to say Iceland's Silvia Night has made a bit of a splash since she's been in Athens. Actually, when I say "made a bit of a splash" I actually mean "caused a right load of carnage" as she's systematically sought, through X-rated outbursts, publicity-seeking antics and relentless rudeness, to antagonise and alienate all, sundry and some others as well. Except that Silvia Night isn't real at all but quite a clever comic creation. Yet the chorus of boos greeting her tonight indicate that either (i) everyone's not in on the joke or (ii) they don't think the joke's all that funny in the first place. Problem is, Silvia's come very well prepared with a great little song called 'Congratulations' (of course) – which is essentially a song of praise to herself (of course). The performance is a deliberate and carefully constructed monument to bad taste, replete with gimp masks, a golden shower reference, a mini-goosestep and a talky bit where Silvia converses with God on the telephone. But this song is CATCHY! And that performance is, if nothing else, a triumph of sheer nerve and what Londoners would call 'front'. For my money, this would certainly light up the Grand Final in quite an unpredictable and therefore very welcome way.

Sakis and Maria are back to check we're OK. It's televoting time and I've got ten minutes to organise my thoughts as all the entries are recapped and my pen and paper finally produce an evolutionary tree that shows Belgium, Estonia and Finland at the top, Poland, Iceland and Russia just below them, then Monaco and Turkey, followed by Belarus plus either Andorra or the Former Yugoslav Republic of Macedonia. Nor am I distracted by Sakis singing (he can spot a captive audience when he sees one, bless him) or checking whether we're excited again. Then, with the interval act, it seems like Greece are trying to harness a bit of the 'Riverdance' vibe. If they're going to aspire to that sort of level, however, they're going to need significantly clickier shoes.

Just to string things out a bit further, Maria bombards us with a few obscure quiz questions most of us already know the answers to, though missing out the one I'm genuinely curious about. No, not 'how do you spell RSPCA?' I mean the one about the number of Eurovision Song Contest presenters you'd actually re-hire. Then we're shown clips of the fourteen songs that have already gone straight through to the Grand Final and I've got to say, with the exception of Romania's 'Tornero', I can't see any of them going toe to toe with the cream of the crop we've seen tonight. I'd place Belgium, Estonia and Finland out on their own and, more than that, by a curious paradox I have a suspicion that this year's Semi-Final is actually stronger than the Grand Final's going to turn out to be. There's still time for Sakis to plug the souvenir DVD and CD before a human chain of volunteers, at long, long last, send the ten crucial envelopes down to the stage from on high (possibly Mount Olympus, if Hephaestus managed to extinguish his flaming gloves in the end).

After a few inter-presenter high jinks with the envelopes – and boy we all needed that, didn't we? – eventually we get down to business. First envelope opens – Russia! Great. No complaints there. Pointless ballet will grace the Grand Final. Second envelope – the Former Yugoslav Republic of Macedonia. Third – Bosnia-Herzegovina. Fourth – Lithuania, greeted by a few boos.

Right, now I'm just starting to get the jitters. Only six envelopes to go and there just aren't enough for all my anointed entries. Fifth – FINLAND! Thank God! Things are turning my way! No, they're not. Ukraine, Ireland and Sweden all pop out in slow succession. Only two places are left now. In the green room, Sandra Oxenryd from Estonia looks exactly like I feel. And I think Kate Ryan from Belgium probably feels exactly how I look. Because now I'm seriously palpitating...

Sakis helpfully reminds us that this is the most crucial and exciting time of the evening. Yes, I'd definitely got that bit. Ninth envelope. Turkey! So now it's a question of everyone clamouring for the final space on the raft. Belgium, Estonia, Poland, Iceland – not to mention Belarus, Monaco and Andorra. Isn't this the bit where Eurovision's Executive Supervisor Svante Stockselius is supposed to intervene and say it's all been a ghastly mistake? Or has the whole evening actually been an inverted travesty of Darwin's survival of the fittest – sort of a process of unnatural selection?

So which one of my favourites will survive the cull? Which one will walk away mentally scarred but musically unscathed having grabbed that last lifejacket? To which one will my other favourites say a simple, valedictory "you go on without me, I'd only slow you down..."?

None of them! Armenia get it! Did Sakis actually shake his head? I know I did. A fireball has appeared from the sky. It's crashed into my Eurovision Earth. The S-F M-T mass extinction event just happened. Right before my eyes. Seven of my favourites wiped out in a flash! And OK, I know that, eventually perhaps, I may just about get over it.

But at the very least you'll have to give me four hundred and forty-five million years.

Bouncing Back

Let me talk to you about your big entrance. No, really. I mean how do you like to create an unforgettable first impression when you sweep into a room? Or when you're at a job interview?

I'm talking about that very first sight they get of you – you know, before it all begins to unravel. And before you resort to deluding yourself that you've started to pull it round. Like when the interviewers ask you what your biggest weakness is. And you say: "if anything, I may be a bit too much of a perfectionist and sometimes, possibly, I may if anything overdo the 'team player' bit." Still, I suppose that's a whole lot better than telling the truth. In life (and especially in the workplace, prospective or actual) honesty's very rarely the best policy. For instance, on balance it's probably best not to tell your prospective employers about your 'funny' ringtones or your habit of breaking wind and then exclaiming "GET IN!" in open-plan offices.

It's also unlikely to be a good idea to take your grandmother to the interview with you. Yet, in effect, that's precisely what Moldova did for their first-ever Eurovision appearance. This was in the 2005 Semi-Final, making it (to all intents and purposes) a job interview for the country. If I spoke any Moldovan (and I won't even claim I can 'get by' or that I'm a bit rusty, even though I might well be tempted to do so in the section on Language Skills in a job application form), I might have had an inkling of what was in store. The title of Zdob şi Zdub's 'Boonika Bate Dobe' actually meant 'Grandmamma Beats the Drum'. So you certainly couldn't accuse them of withholding any vital information.

For me, out of all the debut entries delivered by the torrent of 'new' countries that joined the Eurovision family in the nineties and noughties, this was comfortably the most enjoyable and easily the most memorable. Not a hint of playing it safe, playing the percentages or opting for the long game here. None of that 'maybe we should just do a nice power ballad and ease ourselves in, after all if it's good enough for Glennis Grace this year it's got to be good enough for us' nonsense. No, just a supercharged, nerveless fusion of, well, of almost everything actually as the five-piece band go for the musical equivalent of those cliff-diving competitions where you pray the contestants have the skills not just in terms of plunging a hundred feet off sharp rocks into a narrow inlet of water, but also in terms of reading the tide tables correctly.

In fact, at first, you don't really notice the rocking chair at the back of the set. Nor indeed its occupant. It's only about forty seconds into the song that the words "I think there's an old lady on the stage wearing full national costume" pop into your head. But she and her furniture are probably just part of the furniture, so to speak. And there's so much going on right across the stage, right from the off, that the possibilities for granny-based intervention are a long way from your thoughts. OK, she's got a great big drum on her lap. But who among us can honestly say that this sort of thing wasn't a regular sight at all our family gatherings when we were young? Perhaps she's only here as part of some sort of care in the community programme, or it may be something to do with securing European Union Regional Development Funds for potentially affiliated nations.

Make no mistake – this is an awesome performance by a brilliant band and granny's surely just grateful to have got out of the house and to be having a nice sit down, stranded here among those nice boys whooping and leaping all over the place. But as the last half-minute arrives, there she is! Grandmamma is centre stage, she's beating that drum – and she's pretty happy about it too. Has Eurovision just found its most iconic happy drummer ever? That, I think we need to conclude, is a very real possibility. In fact, Grandmamma's beating the big drum with one hand and clattering

155

a small cymbal on top of it with the other – and now she's doing a series of full twirls! She must be on the fish-oil tablets. Sensational stuff. Quite marvellous. Now THAT'S how a country should arrive at the Eurovision Song Contest and make that all-important first impression absolutely indelible. Even my big entrance can't compare with that.

In some ways, though, making a good first impression can be considerably simpler than creating a good second or subsequent impression, when you've already developed a bit of baggage and, as a result, you might have to fight hard to dispel preconceptions about what a typical entry from, say, the French or the Swiss will entail. Indeed, the whole concept of bouncebackability is a really important one in Eurovision – or at least for any country aspiring to win the contest. Actually, I'd go a lot further than that. Perhaps nothing embodies the spirit of Eurovision better than the ability of a country to come back swinging after a disaster or a drubbing – such as a lamentable last place, a 'nul points' fiasco or an inept elimination at the Semi-Final stage.

I love a good Lazarus-style comeback – and a good Eurovision Lazarus-style comeback most of all. So I'm very definitely not talking here about the sort of 'dead cat bounce' you see in financial markets, where a precipitous plummet is followed by a small recovery basically because the markets simply couldn't fall any further. No. I'm talking about a proper bouncy ball bounce – the kind you get when you ping one of those little hard-rubber balls onto the crazy paving and it whistles up past your face before pinging round the garden in random zigzags and disappears through a rip in the space-time continuum behind the *Euonymus alatus*, immune to discovery regardless of the number of rummages through the undergrowth aimed at bringing it to light again.

Appropriately enough, the first Eurovision star with a compelling claim to gold-plated Eurovision rubber ball status was no less a luminary than Lys Assia herself. In 1956, with uncompromising back-up in the shape of a five-piece close harmony group for whom failure clearly wasn't an option, Lys expertly piloted her way through 'Refrain' – a classic cosy fireplace of a song, though arguably not casting too much more than a modest glow over those who gathered round it – and took the inaugural Eurovision title for Switzerland. Lys returned the following year to defend her title, with 'L'Enfant que J'Étais' ('The Child that I Was'), a song very much chiselled from the same sentimental sedimentary rock.

On this occasion, though, the fickle finger of fate pointed away from Lys or arguably jabbed upwards in her general direction as she came home equal eighth out of ten. Only Austria's Bob Martin (that's right) finished below her with 'Wohin, Kleines Pony?' ('Where to, Little Pony?'), which I assume was only a rhetorical question but, if not, I do have several helpful suggestions. Yet fair play to Lys as she was back again in 1958 (as we've already seen) with the vastly chirpier 'Giorgio' – a song that, looking back at Eurovision through the wrong end of the telescope, actually has all the hallmarks of quite a bold entry. A 1950s 'Boonika Bate Dobe', I'd like to say, with a certain amount of hyperbole. It wasn't quite enough to send Lys boinging over the neighbour's fence but it still secured the runner-up spot – and no individual in Eurovision history would ever (or surely will ever) come as close as Lys to realising a remarkable top-to-bottom-to-top sequence, tracing a line like one of those parabola graphs that clever people with wiry hair look at and pretend they understand.

Lys's nemesis in 1957 had been the Dutch, who posted the first of their four victories in that year with Corry Brokken's 'Net Als Toen' ('Just Like Then'), which for all its period charm could probably never be fairly described as a quantum leap forward from 'Refrain'. Curiously, Corry immediately suffered almost precisely the same fate as Lys, though going one 'better' by finishing equal last in 1958. Yet the Dutch, their flag now borne aloft by Teddy Scholten with "'n

Beetje', achieved that first-last-first triptych that had barely eluded the Swiss. With its 'Calling All Workers' feel, Teddy's song conjures up quite comforting visions of 1950s factory workers traipsing off on foggy mornings to do a ten-hour stint on a noisy production line. And boy did Corry and many of those other early Eurovision contestants not only know how to perform but also how to work a camera, despite those still being pioneering, feel-your-way days of TV.

Sometimes, however, as the Dutch were to prove much later, comebacks can take a little longer. One of the very few downsides to the introduction of Semi-Finals into Eurovision has been its opening up of all kinds of spectacular ways of achieving diabolical failure. These are very public job interviews with a binary hire-or-fire outcome. But at least you get to apply again next year. So when in 2005 Glennis Grace proved Too Far Ahead of Her Time/Too Good for Eurovision, a chance for the Dutch to set the record straight duly arrived the following May. And the May after that. And the May after that too. Indeed, for the next four Mays after that one as well. That's right. Eight Semi-Finals in a row. Zero qualifications for the Grand Final. An unwanted record. Even pushing the emergency blue button marked 'Smurf' didn't deliver the goods as the retro, lightweight but curiously catchy 'Ik Ben Verliefd (Sha-la-lie)' ('I'm in Love') written by Pierre Kartner, a.k.a. Father Abraham, came up short in 2010.

But as the old saying goes, the darkest hour is just before the dawn; in other words, when it's really dark and, if you've got any sense, you're still in bed anyway. Fortunately the Dutch had remembered to set their alarms for 2013 and the excellent Anouk delivered a magnificent wakey-wakey call in the shape of 'Birds', which flew through the Semi-Final and then found a perch just inside the Top Ten on the Saturday. Indeed, the ninth place it achieved was the Netherlands' best finish since the previous millennium. But this was ultimately a comeback destined to be achieved in two big leaps

158

rather than one giant bound and, when the 2014 contest came round, the Dutch next pushed the button marked 'Country & Western – Use Only with Extreme Caution – Please Wear a Hat'. Boy-girl and half-hatted duo The Common Linnets with their insistent, slow-burning but extremely sure-footed 'Calm After the Storm' breezed into second place in the Grand Final, squeezed between Austria's Conchita and Sweden's Sanna Nielsen as few perhaps are. Imagine just what they'd have achieved if BOTH of those Linnets had done the hat thing.

*　　*　　*　　*　　*　　*

The Netherlands don't have a monopoly of Low Country bounce-backs. No, sir. In the mid-1980s, neighbours Belgium provided an absolutely textbook example. Now, on one level Belgium are hardcore Eurovision high flyers in the sense that only Germany, France and the UK have participated in more Eurovisions than them. In terms of results, though, it's been a bit more of a struggle and this is certainly a country that's experienced a decent slab of travesty trouble. Not a description you'd necessarily apply to their 1985 travails, however. 'Laat Me Nu Gaan' ('Let Me Go Now'), with its theme of breaking free and walking away, was a success only in the sense that clearly none of the voting juries were going to stand in Linda Lepomme's way, wherever she was off to. I was going to say (tritely) that it was an unremarkable ballad that unremarkably finished last. But that's a little unfair. It just sounded like a tune lifted out of context from a workmanlike musical called something like 'Chess without the Really Good Choons'.

But far from walking away from Eurovision, Belgium went away, got a complete, empowering makeover and came back fighting. In fact, as a Eurovision-competing country, they got the equivalent of a new haircut, eye-colour-changing contact lenses and dental veneers as they changed tack totally for 1986 and sent thirteen-year-old Sandra Kim into the fray in Bergen. 'J'Aime la Vie' ('I Love Life')

159

certainly did the trick, securing victory through the simple strategy of replacing angst and sober reflection with bounciness, boppiness and a cracking set of synth drums, in what perhaps might best be seen now as a kind of dry run for the Junior Eurovision Song Contest. For Belgium, then, it was thirty-first time lucky and I'd like to think that (a) Fud Leclerc clicked his fingers and tucked into a celebratory Liège meatball (the world's greatest meatballs, since you ask) and (b) Telex were too cool to care.

Because these, surely, are the true heroes of Eurovision, the countries that plug away year after year with little to show for it except for, at best, mild disdain from other nations and, at worst, total unawareness that they'd even been participating in the contest in any case. Quite simply, without the no-hopers and the never-wases, what would Eurovision be – apart from a much shorter evening? No, it takes a truly phenomenal level of grit and resilience to bounce back after literally years and indeed decades of hurt and not only set yourself up for more of the same but actually turn the world upside down and pull off a shock win.

*   *   *   *   *   *

I'm told there used to be a (possibly spurious) joke doing the rounds in Finland that went something like this. A genie appears to a Finnish man and tells him he can have whatever his heart most desires. The Finnish man thinks for a moment and replies that he'd like the region of Finnish Karelia to be removed from Russia and given to Finland. The genie points out that this may not be too straightforward and maybe the man has another suggestion. The Finnish man takes another moment to think and then replies that he'd love Finland, just once, to win the Eurovision Song Contest. "Mmm..." says the genie. "Can I have another look at that map?"

From the point when they joined the Eurovision whirligig in 1961, even modest success perpetually remained a shimmering mirage for the Finns. In fact, the heady heights of sixth place in 1973, courtesy of Marion Rung's underrated and effervescent 'Tom Tom Tom', would prove to be as good as it was ever going to get in the second millennium. Even the double punch of 'Reggae OK' in 1981 and the sage advice that you could probably best survive a nuclear holocaust by having a lie-in delivered by 'Nuku Pommiin' ('Sleep to the Bomb') in 1982 – both personal favourites of mine – failed to achieve anything apart from giving me two more travesties to whinge about as they slumped to sixteenth and a *'nul points'* eighteenth place respectively.

Just when Finland probably thought their Eurovision fortunes couldn't plunge much lower, however, the European Broadcasting Union added a whole new layer to the Victoria sponge of potential humiliation by introducing the concept of relegation to the contest in 1993. With the 'new' countries emerging from the break-up of Yugoslavia and the dissolution of the Soviet Union and its attendant bloc now beginning to rush towards the elevator, the EBU immediately stuck a sign over the contest saying 'maximum load – 25 countries'. Relegation may have represented a sensible way of managing the crush, but almost inevitably Finland regularly finished towards the bottom end of the Grand Final scoreboard, meaning they'd have to kick their heels for a year before being readmitted – only then to finish towards the bottom end of the scoreboard again and miss the following year's contest in a kind of Eurovision Groundhog Day. So Eurovision somehow had to swim Finn-less in 1995, 1997, 1999, 2001 and 2003. Indeed, to all intents and purposes, this annual celebration of song actually became a biennial event for Finland.

Even the admirably inclusive step of introducing a Semi-Final into the process in 2004 only partly alleviated their plight. So in that year and the next, although the Finnish entry was able to appear on the midweek big stage, Saturday remained resiliently Finn-free. Basically, Finland got to eat its burger and fries from a bag, standing outside the fast-food restaurant while looking in through the window at all those who'd managed to bagsy a table. Yet to their enormous credit, they still kept hammering away as they continued to stroll round and round the restaurant in the hope they'd spot someone who was about to leave and then be able to ask one of the restaurant crew to give the table a quick wipe before plonking themselves down at it and finally coming in from the cold.

And unsurprisingly, when Lordi rolled up in 2006 sporting their stunning array of horror and gore-inspired foam latex monster masks plus matching costumes, some of the tables freed up pretty damn quickly. The outcome was not simply a long overdue and appropriately supersized victory but also the re-christening of a square in Mr Lordi's home town of Rovaniemi in honour of the event. Lordi's Square – that's got a real ring to it, hasn't it? And I'd like to think plans were at least discussed to rename one of the roads leading into it Bounce-Back Boulevard.

*   *   *   *   *   *

In recent Eurovision history, there have perhaps been no countries more in need of a stunning comeback than the Big Four or, since 2011, the Big Five – automatic qualifiers for the Grand Final basically by dint of the scale of the readies they place in the European Broadcasting Union's coffers. But whatever France, Germany, Italy, Spain and the UK have gained from not having to subject themselves to the indignity of scrambling for votes in the Semi-Finals, it's generally been counterweighed by their regular visits to the wrong end – and in quite a few cases the very wrong end – of the scoreboard.

Indeed, by the time the 2009 contest had been and gone, it seemed like hell wouldn't just need to freeze over but also successfully submit a bid to host the Winter Olympics before any of the Big Four could entertain serious thoughts of winning the contest again. Germany's plight was pretty typical: twenty-fourth in 2005, fourteenth in 2006, nineteenth in 2007, twenty-third in 2008. Even the on-stage presence of Dita von Teese in 2009 couldn't propel the intriguingly named and vastly entertaining 'Miss Kiss Kiss Bang' any higher than twentieth, just five spots above bottom-placed Finland (for whom normal Eurovision service had now pretty much resumed, as slightly irritable rap consigned Waldo's People to a scandalously low finish for their excellent 'Lose Control').

I'd like to think someone in Germany with psychic powers was already considering the potential saleability of German Eurovision t-shirts incorporating a pleasing parabola design, even as Lena's 'Satellite' was taking shape and swinging into Europe's field of vision in the run-up to the 2010 contest in Oslo. Mangled vowels only added to the charm and the outcome was a deserved landslide victory marking Germany's first since Nicole's triumph just the small matter of twenty-eight years earlier. Comeback complete. Critics confounded. Vowels eviscerated. Job done.

Twenty-eight years. That's seven World Cup cycles. In fact, it's only 6.666 (recurring) percent shorter than the Thirty Years War. It's a long time to wait. But, in mathematical terms, it's still significantly shorter than forty-eight years. Forty-eight years! That's twelve World Cup cycles. It's one year for every hour you'd be awake if you didn't go to bed for two straight days. That's not really very helpful, is it? But you get the idea. Forty-eight years can drag by if there's not a great deal happening.

And in terms of things happening at Eurovision, that was exactly the sad experience of Austria after Udo Jürgens had beaten off the opposition with quite a bit to spare back in 1966. 'Merci, Chérie' ('Thank You, Darling') had put Ireland's Dickie Rock, the UK's Kenneth McKellar and fifteen other pretenders firmly in their place in Luxembourg City, twelve months after France Gall had ratcheted Eurovision up another notch or six with the iconic and instantly memorable 'Poupée de Cire, Poupée de Son' ('Wax Doll, Singing Doll').

After this brief and brilliant intrusion by the Swinging Sixties, Udo's win represented something of a recalibration of the Eurovision clock and a reaffirmation of traditional Eurovision values, with his undemanding but nicely arranged piano-led ballad providing the dictionary definition of the safe winner. What the Austrians couldn't have known, though, as they began to turn their minds to bringing the contest to Vienna in 1967, was that they'd just entered the biggest between-wins trough in Eurovision history.

Possibly the best compliment I can pay to Austria's track record during that period is that at least they had the sense to sidestep the song I submitted to them for the 1985 contest. As it turned out, the entry that beat me, Gary Lux's 'Kinder Dieser Welt' ('Children of This World'), was definitely one of their superior efforts in an era when too many of their entries fell into either the TMM (Too Many Mullets) trap, the TMB (Too Many Ballads) trap, or both. 'Mrs Caroline Robinson' is, of course, exempted from any criticism whatsoever.

One thing you CAN say for Austria, though, is that they certainly know how to field a contestant with a cracking name. Waterloo & Robinson set the bar pretty high in 1976 and then The Rounder Girls gave it another upwards nudge in 2000. But even these fade away into a twilight of nothingness compared with Austria's 2012 model, hip-hop/rap duo Trackshittaz. Their poledance-heavy entry 'Woki mit Deim Popo' ('Waggle Your Butt') didn't lack for talking points but hedonism clearly wasn't too high on Eurovision's hit list that year and the boys technically finished last in the entire competition. I think their entry was an ironic critique on the difficult issue of sexual objectification but it may actually just have been a very rude song.

Nor had regular bouts of non-participation done much to help Austria build up a head of steam. Fifth place finishes had been the summit of their achievement in the fallow years and even then you had to trawl back through the archives to 1989 to find the last one of those. 2013 had seen yet another of those Semi-Final eliminations. So when, early in 2014, the Eurovision fansites started buzzing with the news that, following back-to-back Semi-Final disasters, Austria had placed their trust in a 'bearded lady' with another great name, Conchita Wurst, it was very hard not to come to the initial conclusion that the country's 'more of the same' setting was still in full force.

How wrong I was. In the shape of Conchita, Eurovision had actually found one of its most iconic Eurovision winners of all time – indeed, one of the rare Eurovision victors to achieve genuine cut-through into the wider public consciousness, and not just because 'Rise Like a Phoenix' proved to be a perfectly staged, brilliantly sung power ballad of a calibre rarely heard and seen anywhere, let alone at Eurovision. No, in Conchita, Austria had actually unearthed an artiste of genuine charisma and star quality and with something to say that was genuinely worth hearing. A great debut album also cemented the notion that we'd be hearing and seeing a lot more of Conchita in the future.

So let's give her due credit and due recognition as Conchita, Comeback Queen of Eurovision, who enabled her country to reverse its near-half-century-long plunge into Eurovision also-ran-dom and boing back up into the stratosphere. And when The Makemakes then unfortunately fell back to earth in 2015, finishing pointless alongside the equally luckless Germany at the foot of the pile, Austria joined the even more exclusive down-up-down Eurovision Parabola Club. Which, for my money, isn't a bad effort at all. And is definitely worth a t-shirt.

* * * * * *

But it really would be dereliction of duty not to sign off this chapter by celebrating Portugal's extraordinary victory in 2017, delivered by the remarkable Salvador Sobral and his back-to-basics classic 'Amar Pelos Dois'. This was a case of the world not so much turned upside down as turned inside out. For Portugal, it was forty-ninth time lucky. Let me just repeat that, in case you missed it. Forty-_**NINTH**_ time lucky. A nation widely dismissed and derided as Eurovision no-hopers. A nation which probably barely even registered with most viewers most years. A nation whose Eurovision fate was surely this: to be served up as so much Semi-Final fodder, painful year after painful year after painful year with a bit of extra agony thrown in.

The lesson is clear. When it comes to Eurovision, if at first you don't succeed, dig in, keep smiling and give it half a century.

Postcard: Saturday 3rd April 1976

Who was it who once said that someone who never learns, never learns to be someone? No, I don't know either. But I certainly take the point that, as we chart the narrow and uncertain course of our lives, we pick up all sorts of handy stuff that can come in really quite useful later on.

To take just one example, there is of course the key life lesson about never losing a receipt, but always pretending you've lost the receipt if it's tactically advantageous to you to do so. Like when you've bought someone a 'that'll do' present and they slip into conversation within five minutes of opening it that it's just what they wanted but ideally they'd have liked a different colour, the next size up, one with a slightly wider nozzle, bigger aperture etc etc etc – and would you mind just popping back to the shop where you got it and exchanging it for a different one etc etc etc. Nor should you forget the option of just creating a smudgy grey area by mentioning that you MAY possibly still have the receipt, but without finally committing yourself until you've incontrovertibly established whether admitting to its existence could end up inconveniencing you personally. Complicated things, receipts.

Eurovision, as you'd only expect, teaches us several valuable life lessons. First and foremost, always try to be Swedish. There can be enormous advantages. If you don't realise what these are, you really are reading the wrong book. Secondly, translating presenter-spiel into both English and French really is unlikely to win many people over to your side. Thirdly, ballads may win you contests but they can also lose you friends. Fourthly, finally and most importantly of all, never, ever, EVER sing the word 'hippety' in any sort of proximity to the title of your song if the title of your song is 'Pump-Pump'. (In much the same way as you really shouldn't ever place the word 'luscious' right in front of the word 'thighs', regardless of the example set by Latvia's Musiqq in 2011.) If the worst SHOULD happen, certainly make sure you're not thrusting your hips forward and back at the time. Having said that, if you're from Finland, you may well get away with it. That was perhaps the key lesson we learnt during the course of the 1976 Eurovision Song Contest.

Oh and it was quite a big night for Brotherhood of Man too.

*   *   *   *   *   *

Good grief, has it really been a year since Teach-In dinged, danged and donged their way to Eurovision victory in Stockholm with 'Ding Dinge Dong'? As a result, the contest bandwagon has rolled into The Hague – the seat of Dutch government and, if we take the opening travelogue at its word, a perfect place for a space disco. So good news for all you Hawkwind fans who've tuned in tonight. Even better than that, the Metropole Orchestra are in position and – wait! Look! It's only Corry Brokken! Yes, the compering tonight is in the hands of genuine Eurovision royalty as the first-ever Dutch winner of the contest, a little matter of nineteen years ago, is going to guide us through tonight's rapids with just a big pair of standard issue 1970s glasses and a rolled-up piece of paper to assist her. Not sure what's on the piece of paper. Perhaps there are some late football results we need to be brought up to speed on. Maybe there's been a late equaliser at Ajax. And Corry does indeed want to talk numbers with us, claiming that four hundred and fifty million people in thirty-three countries will be watching eighteen nations slugging it out for the title tonight here in the Congresgebouw in the shadow of the cleverly shape-shifting set. I wonder if it can turn into a Viking longship?

Talking of which, there's no Sweden this year. After hosting the contest last year and winning with ABBA the year before that, it seems a strange absence. I believe it's a cocktail of financial and other reasons that's to blame but it still feels a little like taking to the field for a major cup final without your captain, who's decided to stay in to wash (and possibly peroxide) his hair and then probably write a million-selling song about it.

The good news from the UK's point of view, though, is that there'll be no nervous hanging around backstage waiting to perform tonight as it's Brotherhood of Man who've been drawn in the get-it-over-and-done-with slot. The preceding postcard shows the foursome strolling on London's Embankment sporting plastic London bobby helmets before decamping to Trafalgar Square. Yes, that's Martin Lee, Lee Sheriden, Nicky Stevens and Sandra Stevens. Remember, this is the crisis-what-crisis 1970s so Britain's name shortage is clearly starting to bite. But arguably it's not so much the song, 'Save Your Kisses for Me', that's the star here. No, it's the routine and specifically the steppy dance presumably honed while trying to avoid letting those massive flares trail in those London puddles. Top marks, too, to the orchestra's piano player who's obviously in a rich vein of form at the moment.

The song ends to healthy applause, bouquets are brought out and there's literally nothing more that Brotherhood of Man can do to influence the outcome tonight – except perhaps rewire tonight's electronic scoreboard to ensure that all their points are doubled and no-one else's appear at all. I suppose it might also be possible to do that thing they do with pocket calculators and get the scoreboard to display electronic numbers upside down that spell out the word 'GOOLIES'. But it's hard to see how that might be turned directly to the UK's advantage. Though I'm working on it.

Ah, the old sad clown routine. Switzerland's Peter, Sue and Marc, returnees from the 1971 contest, have brought us 'Djambo, Djambo' this time round. I assume that's the name of the clown who's dividing his time between a barrel organ and an acoustic guitar. He certainly looks like he's got the hump about something but, frankly, I think he needs to get a grip and be thankful for the work. It's actually not an unpleasant song in its US West Coast sort of way, despite Djambo's best efforts at dragging the mood down. And when the flowers come on at the end, there are none at all for the clown. Quite right too. You really don't want to be seen to be rewarding that kind of behaviour.

Now this year Germany have gone for an interesting variation on the 'enter a song that might have won last year' tactic. They've actually gone a step further by entering a song with almost exactly the same title. 'Sing Sang Song' is being performed by the Les Humphries Singers (a good old Westphalian name, presumably). Although Les himself, neck girded with literally the world's best cravat, will actually be doing the conducting while his six-piece vocal harmony outfit do all the sing, sang, songing. And what a rum bunch they make, as it looks a bit like the look-alike agency has played a key role in pulling the group together. So from left to right we've got: Three Degrees lady, New Seekers lady, Mud man, Marc Bolan, someone from Crosby, Stills & Nash (not sure which one) and an Osmond brother (again, not sure which one). Oh and there's a quick kiss for New Seekers lady from Mud man. I wonder if they're all available for summer season? Having said that, this entry is the sort of nonsense that I quite enjoy and there's flowers for the girls and for Marc Bolan too as this jolly little curio finally runs into the buffers.

Israel's perky trio Chocolate, Menta, Mastik then spend the full three minutes trying to out-perk each other as their song 'Emor Shalom' ('Say Hello') breaks out from an intro that has a whiff of the why-why-Delilahs about it and settles down into quite a spirited groove enhanced by some decent brass work from the orchestra. And here in their slipstream comes Jürgen Marcus for Luxembourg, with a steady piano intro setting up his French ballad 'Chansons pour Ceux qui s'Aiment' ('Songs for Those Who Love Each Other'). Now Jürgen's got impressively wide hair – collectively, I mean, not in terms of the individual strands – and a quick flick of the head shows just how well it holds its shape. He's also got a penchant for throwing his arms out wide with panache, especially as the chorus kicks in with a marching- band feel. It's all quite likeable and confident, although I'll have forgotten it again in a minute. Thinking about it, does French have a word for 'penchant'? Or indeed for 'panache'?

Here's someone called Pierre Rapsat who's going to sing for Belgium. In his postcard, Pierre lurks around the Atomium and the Grand Place in Brussels in a big fur coat, which is his democratic right of course. His song 'Judy et Cie' ('Judy & Company') looks like it's going to be a moody one. Pierre's got a twelve-string acoustic guitar, which I guess means there's more chance of more of them being in tune, and he's also got a capo on the ninth fret, which is the sort of thing that interests me but probably not you. As for his lapels, they're so wide you could get planning permission to build a small retail park on them, with generous provision for mother-and-child parking spaces. Again, though, joking apart, I quite like this song. I wonder if back home Pierre's dubbed the Brussels Bedsit Balladeer? And what's this? The welcome return of Operation Whistle! Excellent. I wouldn't say this has got much chance of winning, but it would make a great album track on one of those albums you don't actually play very much.

Red Hurley's green velvet suit is, for me, the big conversation piece during this year's Irish entry, the big and slightly James Bond-y 'When'. Excellent piece of cloth. Strangely, this is a song that sounds like it should be in French for maximum effect, with its slightly plaintive, lovelorn nature. Wouldn't it be great if we found out that all these guys tonight singing ballads of hurt and regret were actually singing about the same girl? (Judy, presumably. I wonder if it's the same one Tommy Körberg had a run-in with in 1969?) And wouldn't it be great if this only became clear to them when they were all backstage and then a big ruck broke out? Again, maybe it's just me. And there's certainly no hint of Judy in the

Dutch entry 'The Party's Over Now', sung by Sandra Reemer. Having utilised her little preview postcard to highlight the possibilities presented by multi-coloured knitwear, Sandra then covers her body in grey chiffon gauze to unleash an interesting two-paced song that seems to give a bit of a nod towards Mary Hopkin's 'Those Were the Days', with wistful violin and street-organ stylings fleshing things out a little.

But the party's definitely not over just yet – at least not if Norway's Anne-Karine Strøm has any influence on the matter. And the matter in question is 'Mata Hari', a song namechecking the infamous World War One spy who got shot for her shenanigans. Well, sing a song of international reconciliation, that's what I say. This is Anne-Karine's third crack at the contest and I can't say I'm massively hopeful about her chances. It's jolly in an upbeat, up-for-a-boogie way but its appeal is being kept a closely guarded secret, which is ironic really, given its subject matter. Full marks for the gold catsuit, though, nicely set off by a headband and a big pair of '70s shades. No, the shades are off again. And now they're on again. And off again. But they're back on for the end of a song that I reckon Anne-Karine may think has gone a bit better than it actually has.

Now here's the type of song I wouldn't usually like but in this case I sort of do. Greece are fielding Mariza Koch and the powerful, unflinchingly Greek protest song 'Panaghia Mou, Panaghia Mou' ('Country of Mine, Country of Mine') which apparently she wrote herself. She's accompanied by a great big bouzouki but my ear's caught more by the prog-rock keyboard line layered over the top. I AM LOVING THAT SYNTH. Looking beyond that, though, it's unarguable that Mariza's got (a) a voluminous black dress and (b) a song with a message. Not speaking much Greek (I'm a bit rusty), I've no idea what that message is. It's obviously not 'have you considered singing in English?' As the song moves towards its conclusion, what sound like cymbal or possibly gong crashes make noises like a New Jersey steelworks and everything's been steered successfully towards its big finish.

While we're on the subject of big Finnish – Finland's Fredi is definitely at the large-boned end of the spectrum of human morphology and he's brought the Friends with him to sing a song with a PROPER Eurovision Song Contest title: 'Pump-Pump'. Maybe it's going to be about waste water treatment in the Helsinki suburbs. Ah, no it's not. I suppose I should have suspected something might be amiss when the Finnish conductor took to the podium and flicked a quick V-sign at the first violins. (On reflection, maybe he was just signalling 'two beats in', like that could possibly be important in a song called 'Pump-Pump'.)

After another slightly Delilah-esque opening, it's over to Fredi whose glittering lapels on his velvet jacket make him look a little like a Lord Mayor. In his mayoral retinue, he's got three girls in pink and one man in compulsory '70s 'tache and tank-top and they've now found their way towards the thing I most feared: a chorus where the song title is preceded by the word 'hippety' and accompanied by hip thrusts. That surely won't help his chances of re-election to mayoral office if the papers get hold of it. Fair play, though – Fredi & the Friends all seem pretty enthusiastic about the whole proposition. Must be something to do with those long, cold Finnish nights and the *aurora borealis*. But this is supreme, only-at-Eurovision stuff. Dumb fun at its (im)purest and its most appealing. It should be compulsory viewing for Djambo the clown, for starters. And also for anyone about to participate in key arms reduction negotiations. Lighten up, world! This is the kind of song that could thaw a Cold War.

Spanish singer Braulio, meanwhile, looks a bit like a young Billy Joel or Jasper Carrott, or possibly the Spanish Lovejoy. In fact, like most if not all of tonight's male contestants, his look and appearance perhaps indicate that singing may only be a side line from a day job teaching at a 1970s London comprehensive school. And yes, he's just nipped out for a quick break-time fag during the preview postcard. As the song starts, it's clear that Braulio favours the mike-held-slightly-to-the-side technique perfected by Jack Jones (the crooner, not the head of the Transport & General Workers' Union). And here are the la-la-la's, courtesy of the backing singers. But it's all quite pleasant, confident and measured, and Braulio has a very decent vibrato on him. But the song's not that memorable and, as the obligatory flowers come on at the end, my mind wanders to the question of whether these are different bunches every time or just the same ones being grabbed back from the contestants as they leave the stage and then recycled.

Clowning around in the Colosseum. That's my minimum expectation from any husband-and-wife duo representing Italy at the Eurovision Song Contest. And as the postcard fades away and the orchestra hits the 'go' button, here comes Romina Power, walking on from the left-hand side of the stage and singing in English. And here comes red-suited Al Bano, walking on from the right-hand side of the stage and singing in Italian. They've clearly agreed to meet at the big red spot in the centre of the stage and this they do brilliantly. That's what just a little bit of planning and some decent timekeeping can do for you. The song's all about living it all again but, personally, I'm struggling a touch with it and wouldn't really want to live it all again, given the choice.

Let's press on. Rather marvellously, Austria's song is to be conducted by a Dr Kleinschuster. (I wonder if there's such a thing as 'Dr K' orthopaedic footwear?) I'd say Dr Kleinschuster's doctorate means he might be just a little overqualified for this Eurovision conducting lark as this entry definitely falls into the 'fun' category. Mind you, I'm not really sure why, or indeed if, it's fun. 'My Little World' is being performed by a male duo called Waterloo & Robinson, which to my ears sounds like a health supplement store or possibly a nice shoe shop where they sell a wide range of standard as well as specialist 'Dr K' footwear.

Portugal's effort, on the other hand, is to be performed by someone else in need of a fag at break time, or that's what the preview postcard seems to indicate. Carlos de Carmo has brought not just a ballad with him but also someone playing a classical guitar and someone playing what we musicians call a mandolin-y thing. This is another song with a French feel in a kind of 'Windmills of My Mind' way, though I think if you turned the sound off and just watched the picture you might very well conclude you were watching Terry Wogan hosting a classic episode of 'Children in Need'. For me, Carlos's song doesn't have a clear sense of direction. But there again, neither does my life so it seems a bit rich for me to make that particular criticism.

Next. Monaco's 'Toi, la Musique et Moi' ('You, Music and Me'), performed by Mary Cristy, sounds like an interesting *ménage à trois* but leaves me a little cold – possibly on account of its somewhat self-conscious breeziness. France's effort looks a lot more promising, though. Called 'Un, Deux, Trois', I'm kind of hoping it's about a cat that sank. And it's going to be sung by Catherine Ferry and you simply have no idea just how much I'm hoping she's got a sister called Britney. I ought to commend the conductor, too, for taking to the rostrum with a cracking red velvet jacket which has helpfully just reminded me to chase up that quote for re-covering our settee. Joking apart, once it parks the 'Puppet on a String' mood of the intro, it's not a bad little song at all – quite a bubbly number reinforced by some neat double handclaps, which are always likely to turn my head, and the crowd clearly concur with me. There you go, Catherine. Have some flowers.

Have we really motored through seventeen songs already? Do we really need an eighteenth? Apparently we do and here are Yugoslavia to deliver it, in the shape of five-guys-one-girl group

Ambassadori. There's some world-class facial hair on show and the female singer's got the kind of flicky hairdo that, as a means of dating a musical performance to the mid-1970s, is a vastly more reliable tool even than carbon dating. And it's always good to see a set of bongos stealing a slice of the limelight. But let me stick my neck right out and say that this song definitely isn't going to win. Anything.

*   *   *   *   *   *

And that, in the most literal sense of the word, is it. Corry's back to opine that the juries have a difficult job on their hands and then the Dutch Swing College Band hawk their Dixieland wares while those juries conduct their deliberations. Truth be told, they'll probably spend the next ten minutes focused on getting some takeaway ordered and sorting through the food once it arrives. "Right, who ordered the dough balls?" But let's go with the fiction for the moment and instead ask ourselves why each of the eighteen juries has eleven members rather than, say, ten or twelve. Is each of them actually a girl's hockey team? Or did they have only hendecagonal tables available for them to sit round?

As the band swings on, they're faded down intermittently to provide a few awkward-interview-sized gaps in which a handful of tonight's contestants are cornered in the green room and asked to namecheck who their favourite is or who they think's going to win. And naturally, they're non-committal or evasive to a fault, except for France's Catherine Ferry who offers a straight question an uncharacteristically straight answer: "Brotherhood of Man."

Generous applause greets the conclusion of the Dutch Swing College Band's set and, as soon as Corry's introduced tonight's Voting Scrutineer (our old amigo Clifford Brown) no less than three times (in Dutch, French and English), it's just about time to chuck some points around.

The UK jury put down the first set of markers. First award – twelve to Switzerland! I see, it's a top-down approach is it this year? No it isn't, as next it's six for Israel. Oh, I get it now – the marks are being given in the order that the countries appear on the scoreboard (in other words the order they sang in). So then it's seven for Belgium, ten for Ireland and then a bunch of others, until we finally get down to eight for France.

Switzerland sound like they're calling in from a mining colony on the dark side of Mercury and seem very keen to get their votes in and go on and do something else with the rest of their evening – possibly divide up those dough balls. But it's the full packet of twelve points for the UK and it soon emerges, as the whole voting process proceeds tonight with exemplary speed and efficiency, that the Brits will be disputing the title with France and, possibly, Monaco. After five juries have had their say, we get a quick backstage glimpse of seventy-five percent of Brotherhood of Man and just Norway are still languishing pointless.

Once we hit the halfway mark, the UK finally nudge ahead of the French with a game in hand, so to speak, as the French jury haven't cast their votes yet and they won't, of course, be able to vote for themselves. And once Spain award the UK twelve and France ten, extending the lead to eleven points, we finally pinpoint all one hundred percent of Brotherhood of Man which possibly indicates the direction of travel.

But it's certainly not finished yet and a quick "woo!" and a "well, well!" from Corry greet the Austrian declaration that leaves France just seven behind the UK. Indeed, it's not until Portugal bump the UK up to a hundred and thirty-seven and only nudge France up to a hundred and twenty-three that Brotherhood of Man finally build up a one-game cushion to add to their game in hand. And when the French provide the evening's penultimate set of points, it really is crunch time. (You can tell that's the case from the fact that the

Norwegian singer's taken her shades off again.) Seven for the UK seals it, the Yugoslavian marks simply reinforce the outcome and, before you know it, it's thumbs up from Brotherhood of Man backstage and Corry's reading off the details of the winning song from a folded piece of paper that's clearly just been ripped from a wire-bound pad of foolscap paper.

Getty Kaspers from Teach-In does the presentation honours, the inevitable flowers are distributed and the music for the reprise comes in a bit sharpish, compelling our winners to chuck the flowers behind them and start what seems, as with ABBA two years ago, an even more relaxed performance facilitated by the heady wine of victory. One of the songwriters has made it to the stage too and is making a slightly odd arm movement, like he's been sleeping on it and is trying to get it going again.

And when it's all wrapped up, Corry says a few words into a dead microphone, there's a quick whistle of feedback and a few noises off, and we're deep into the traditional mild chaos of the closing moments of the Eurovision Song Contest. A stray human hand passes across the screen to move the logo that constitutes the first sheet of credits and that's your lot. The title is the UK's, Finland have pump-pumped their way to lower-mid-table relative respectability and Norway have finished bottom but thankfully without a 'nul points' humiliation.

But what's that sound? I do believe it may be Jahn Teigen just starting to warm up...

Now There's a Novelty

I don't know if you spend a lot of your time among non-initiates. I do. According to the old saying, no man is an island but, as far as Eurovision's concerned, I definitely seem to spend most of the year with water lapping round my feet. And in my experience, non-initiates can be divided pretty neatly into two tribes: those for whom your love of Eurovision whooshes straight over (or possibly clean through) their heads; and those who take your love of Eurovision as cast-iron proof that you know the square root of precisely nothing at all about music.

One innocent mention of the fact that I'm currently listening to Måns Zelmerlöw's debut album in the car, that I've just been re-watching Põhja-Tallinn at the 2013 and 2016 Eesti Laul or that I'll be staying in on Friday evening to re-arrange my Eurovision double CDs not in chronological order but in alphabetical order of host cities is enough to trigger the usual chain reaction of events. First, the confused looks. Next, the facial expressions conveying wry amusement. Then the almost imperceptible shaking of the head that says "why can't he listen to some proper music?" – proper music just happening to coincide exactly, of course, with whatever their music collection happens to consist of and usually revolving around Adele.

Of course, as we all know, the irony is that _they're_ the lost souls; _they're_ the ships cut adrift on the foaming ocean of absence; _they're_ the sheep that have strayed from the Europop pasture and need to be herded back into the pen. Maybe like me you've been confronted by this wall of scorn and this edifice of almost wilful misunderstanding. Maybe like me, on occasion, you've been moved to utter the words that are guaranteed more than any others to prompt a snort of derisive laughter from anyone fully immunised against the Eurovision bacillus: "you really don't know what you're missing…"

The problem is, almost any argument you deploy and almost any point you make to help you build up a case for the Eurovision Song Contest's quality, its credibility and its credentials as a musical event worth exploring will be met with a single-word retort. Moreover, it's a single word that your opponent in debate will see as an absolutely unanswerable refutation of anything and everything you say – the smoking gun that, in their mind, proves they're one hundred percent right and you're one hundred percent wrong. And the word is 'Scooch'.

You see, in the mind of the Eurovision unbeliever, every song in the contest is a novelty song. Every entry is a musical mis-step. In their eyes, Scooch = normal. Or normal for Eurovision. That's what Eurovision is. To boil it down even further, every single song in the contest is a send-up, a wind-up or a cock-up. As far as the unbelievers are concerned, all of Eurovision must be judged and condemned by its association with the perceived lowest lifeform in its gloopy primordial soup of stunted, malformed musical guff. And the lifeform in question is the novelty entry.

But in the empire of Eurovision, what exactly is a 'novelty entry' anyway? Does the performer even have to know or intend it to be a novelty entry for it to be categorised as one? Who gets to apply that damning description? Is there a manual we can look up on the internet to help us decide which songs it applies to? And is an accidental novelty entry every bit as valid as – in addition to probably being slightly more entertaining than – a deliberate novelty entry?

These are the kinds of questions that keep me awake at night more often than I care to admit. In fact, these are also the kinds of questions that used to keep me awake during long meetings, way back in the days when I still did a proper job in the environmental consultancy sector and the fate of the nation seemed to hang on how many wind turbines you could stick up close to an Area of Outstanding Natural Beauty before the local people started to notice or the badgers complained. Your mind could really wander during those meetings, let me tell you.

This isn't an 'us' and 'them' issue either, with Eurovision fans on one side of the argument and non-believers on the other. Because arguably no topic divides the Church of Eurovision itself quite as much as whether novelty entries represent the path to salvation or carry the number of the beast tattooed on the back of their collective neck.

(Just as a quick aside, the number of the beast in Eurovision terms isn't six hundred and sixty-six, of course. It's two – the bogey slot in the Grand Final from which victory is quite literally impossible. The laws of physics simply will not let it happen. Something to do with top quarks and the strong nuclear force, I believe. And anyone seeking to fly in the face of this cosmic truth, from Olivia Newton-John to Jahn Teigen, from Peter, Sue and Marc to Alf Poier, has also had to contend with the four horsemen of the Euro Apocalypse: Pestilence, War, Famine and, most devastating of all, Bloc Voting. Two also represents: the number of times at Eurovision that a band trying to pretend to be 'party people' haven't actually come across like a bunch of complete and utter tools; the number of times an outrageous mullet hasn't seriously detracted attention from the song itself and hasn't also delivered a stark warning of the perils involved in slavishly following current hairstyle fashion; and the number of songs in the whole, fertile, febrile history of Eurovision that have genuinely been enriched by the inclusion of an accordion. In case you're wondering, those two songs are actually referred to later in this very chapter, so hang on in there.)

In the great internal Euro-theological debate about novelty entries, I'm pretty sure I'm in the minority. Yes, I'm on the heretical side of the argument that welcomes the inclusion of a couple of such songs every year. For me, without something inexplicable and possibly inexcusable to chew on, Eurovision is a slightly less appetising event. In my view, variety really is the spice of Eurovision life and there's certainly more than enough spare capacity in a field of forty-odd songs for a bit of ill-judged humour and some questionable taste. The opposite side of the argument, however, maintains that 'funny' entries are a key reason why the Eurovision Song Contest has a bit of a perception problem among big swathes of the wider public – and why some people view us Eurovision fans as a class of hominid lying somewhere between Homo Erectus and Java Man on the human evolutionary tree.

And it's hard to counter the view that, with just a few exceptions, the entries that sear themselves into the public consciousness – as evidenced by those that get held up for scrutiny and ridicule through the medium of short clips played during comedy panel shows, for example – tend to be the ones at the novelty end of the spectrum. Silly costumes. Madmen at play. Schmetterlinge. Dustin the Turkey.

*　　*　　*　　*　　*　　*

In the sphere of Eurovision novelty acts, Ireland's Dustin the Turkey was actually one of the exceptions – and not just because he was a puppet. Appearing in the contest a year after Scooch had crash-landed in 2007, his 'Irelande Douze Pointe' contained actual jokes, just like Scooch's 'Flying the Flag (for You)' had tried to do. How funny those jokes were is another matter altogether, though I quite liked the one about 'Riverdance'. But aside from the obvious point that, as always at Eurovision, it's all in the eye of the beholder and one person's laugh fest is another's lame duck, or one person's affectionate pastiche is another's disrespectful mick-take, it's important to note that what often actually marks out a Eurovision novelty song is not what it sounds like but what it looks like.

182

To take that observation just a little bit further, is it a novelty song – or is it art? Paul Oscar's somewhat infamous Icelandic entry 'Minn Hinsti Dans' ('My Final Dance') from 1997 was hardly a novelty song from either a musical or a lyrical perspective. But you'd have been hard-pressed to ditch that description on the evidence of your own two eyes when you saw Paul sitting on a big white settee, his PVC-clad legs akimbo, awash in a sea of fishnets, stroking a combination of inner thighs (his own), legs (other people's) and crotch (his own again), and leaving you to draw the conclusion that it really is amazing what you can try and get away with if you think of it as art.

Paul, for his pains, got a bit of a mixed reception, as the saying goes. And that's generally been the lot of the novelty entry, in more recent times especially. On some occasions, as we've already seen in the case of Silvia Night, they can even be booed to oblivion. Neither charisma nor stage presence may be enough to win the audience over, but that elusive, indefinable quality called 'charm' just might be.

To take an obvious example, you'd need a heart of flint to catcall or verbally bottle off six dear old grannies who've swung in from Buranovo village in Russian Udmurtia with a massive oven and a message that says 'Party for Everyone' – a party where the provision of an adequate supply of bread-based nibbles presumably won't pose much of a problem. No, there wasn't even a hint of a negative crowd reaction on that occasion in Baku in 2012. Mind you, bearing in mind how freshly baked bread regularly tops 'favourite smell' polls, even to the point of outgunning sizzling bacon, fresh-cut grass and (my own personal favourite) the new Eurovision double CD, maybe the oven was simply an ingenious example of chemical-induced brainwashing on a stadium-sized scale. Cunning grannies.

Similarly, if you'd told me in advance that a man in his early thirties combining a mullet and a balding crown, clad in platforms and a turquoise velvet suit, who then took the time to rub random audience members, stroke and kiss a steward, single out the imperious Katie Boyle in the front row and even find space in his diary for a quick cowbell solo before climbing up some wobbly scaffolding, would finish a creditable seventh – as Germany's Guildo Horn did in 1998 with 'Guildo Hat Euch Lieb!' ('Guildo Loves You!') – I'd have been delighted but nevertheless quite surprised. On the other hand, when a man in his early thirties clad in a yellow leather jacket rapped among a class of five schoolgirls and finished down in nineteenth place – as the UK's Daz Sampson did in 2006 with 'Teenage Life' – I wasn't that surprised. But it was certainly encouraging to see average class sizes coming down, even though Daz looked destined to struggle a bit for supply work as his class control skills didn't seem all that brilliant, to be blunt. Hats off indoors, girls, at the very least.

But was 'Teenage Life' actually a novelty song? Would Daz have claimed it to be one or would he have railed against such a description? And in that same year, did Lordi count as a novelty act? They didn't really for me, possibly because I quite like heavy metal, but what's your take on that one? Are masks and costumes enough to tip the balance? You're almost certainly screaming "of course they are, you muppet!" right now but this may be one of those things where, automatically, the songs you like don't count as novelty entries but, equally automatically, the songs you don't like do.

Having said that, as I've implied, I personally don't see 'novelty song' as a negative term at all. And I'm speaking as someone who was (and still is) the proud owner of the twelve-inch version of the mid-'80s Dutch Euro hit 'Holiday Rap' by MC Miker G and DJ Sven. I'm pretty sure I once also had copies of Benny Hill's 'Ernie (the Fastest Milkman in the West)', Alexei Sayle's 'Ullo John! Gotta New Motor?', Billy Howard's 'King of the Cops' and 'N, N, Nineteen Not

Out' by The Commentators. So novelty songs hold very few terrors for me.

Schmetterlinge seemed to hold quite a few terrors for everyone else in 1977, though. Way beyond spoof, Austria's entry 'Boom Boom Boomerang' fell into the super-spoof or possibly hyper-spoof category but was still likely to give small children sleepless nights and a need for a lifetime of therapy. The gentle *a cappella* intro simply lured the unwary into a strange quagmire where the four boys in the group adopted a different-costumes-on-our-fronts-and-backs-plus-scary-masks-on-the-backs-of-our-heads strategy as Schmetterlinge delivered part puppet show, part lampoon of the music industry with words seemingly provided by a random lyric generator that threw up 'hijack', 'Kojak' and 'didgeridoo', as well as my own personal favourite 'snadderydang'.

But it was 2007, the Chinese year of the Scooch, that saw the art of the novelty Eurovision entry arguably reach its high-water mark. Indeed, the sheer weight of such songs saw the Good Ship Eurovision's Plimsoll line disappear completely from view. You could certainly make a decent case for slapping the novelty label on a good twenty-five percent of the songs in that particular contest, if not more. It was a year of air stewardesses, vampires and drag queens. In short, my kind of party. And the mood was set very early on in the Semi-Final when Israel's Teapacks presented 'Push the Button', their quirky slant on a topic rarely broached at Eurovision and pretty tricky to cover at any time with any element of humour – total nuclear annihilation. Does 'Push the Button' count as a novelty entry, as satire or as acerbic political comment? Can't it be all three at once?

One thing's for sure: the hoo-ha and hullaballoo that attended its selection for the contest was all the proof you could need that it veered miles away from the cosy tramlines of Eurovision conformity and acceptability. And the fact that it delivered a serious message in a wonderfully subversive envelope (underlined by some very clever, very witty lyrics) added nicely to the general disorientation and discomposure the song caused around the Eurovision community. For me personally, what really gave it the hallmark of a vintage offbeat Eurovision entry was the band itself and the humour and irony that ran through their performance. There's a simple equation here that may well be helpful: pipe-smoking accordionist = novelty entry.

2007 is also 'novelty notable' for the fact that a song with as comprehensive a set of novelty credentials as you could ask for came within an ace of winning the contest. Racking up two hundred and thirty-five points in the Grand Final, it finished in second place just thirty-three points adrift of the eventual winner, Serbia's big ballad 'Molitva' ('Prayer'). Performed by a drag character invented by a Ukrainian comedian, 'Dancing Lasha Tumbai' (yet another untranslatable title) arguably made every other spoof song that ever had been or might ever be entered into the Eurovision Song Contest completely obsolete.

Think of it as the Dreadnought of Eurovision novelty entries. It also had the sheer effrontery to incorporate a whole blizzard of brilliant vocal and accordion-led instrumental hooks – and that's even before you factor in how Verka Serduchka presided over a performance of such unreconstructed silver-foiled comic brilliance that the audience was left with simply no alternative other than to raise the roof of Helsinki's Hartwall Areena.

To my eyes, the absolute masterstroke that put the final gloss on this extraordinary once-seen, never-forgotten, oft-cited gamut of genius was the inclusion of a whole welter of dance moves that would grace any over-'60s disco absolutely anywhere in the world. My personal favourite was the little hoppy dance Verka and her cohorts executed expertly a little under a minute into the song. This also had the not unwelcome by-product of bringing back a few memories of another classic novelty entry from precisely twenty years earlier. That was the occasion when white-socked Israeli duo Datner & Kushnir's 'The Bums' Song' provided the vehicle for a relentless barrage of deft and eccentric footwork as part of a routine that represented the closest Eurovision equivalent to a Jim Carrey movie, especially if Jim had ever been roped into an ill-judged remake of 'The Blues Brothers'.

(And yes – you're absolutely correct. 'Dancing Lasha Tumbai' and 'Push the Button' are indeed the two songs I mentioned earlier where the inclusion of an accordion was a genuinely good call. Though I ought to give an honourable mention, too, to Serbia's 'Cipela', or 'The Shoe', from 2009 – a highly entertaining romp that seemed to revolve around an ill-fated wedding ceremony, ultra-curly footwear and a quite magnificent mustard-coloured jacket.)

Since 2007's Verka-led heyday, however, the Eurovision novelty song has gone into something of a spiral of decline. While this is neither total nor terminal, this decline has clearly coincided with the return of jury input to the voting process – leaving us to infer that countries these days believe that 'music professionals' in other countries either (a) have absolutely no sense of humour or (b) see absolutely no artistic merit in anything with verbal or visual jokes in it. I beg to differ, though. Of course, juries won't vote for a bad spoof song. But they don't vote for any sort of bad song. At least not intentionally, I hope. A cleverly conceived, nicely observed and tightly delivered spoof, on the other hand, can be a work of entertainment as well as art – and why couldn't the juries appreciate that? The grannies came in second, after all. A novelty entry is a bit like that Marcel Duchamp creation of the Mona Lisa with a moustache. Not everyone will like it. But it could be worth millions to someone.

* * * * * *

I'm not sure we've made a hell of a lot of progress in pinpointing beyond all reasonable doubt what actually constitutes a Eurovision novelty entry. So let's simply close this chapter by reflecting on the year after Verka came, hopped and almost conquered – the last year before the return of jury voting started to release some of the air from the novelty entry balloon. In a magnificent flurry of Eurovision nonsense, Dustin the Turkey gobbled up alarmingly few votes, Estonia's Kreisiraadio possibly confused themselves as much as everybody else with 'Leto Svet' ('Summer World'), Bosnia-Herzegovina's Laka literally hung the washing out to dry in the glorious 'Pokušaj' ('Try'), while Latvian pirates got themselves marooned on dry land in 'Wolves of the Sea' (though they're still available for kids' parties and garden fêtes, I'd imagine). And that was even before Spain out-spoofed the spoofers with the bold (and booed) 'Baila el Chiki-Chiki' ('Dance the Chiki-Chiki'), a full-on comedy number replete with stumbling, fumbling dancers, a toy guitar and a neat line in robo-dad-dancing.

Yet for me, every last one of these was comfortably put in the shade by a long-haired, bearded Frenchman in sunglasses: driving onto the stage in a golf buggy with a helium-filled inflatable globe under his arm; waving to the crowd before gingerly sort-of-tiptoeing sideways towards them; dodging a whole welter of set camera shots to disappear from view at every inopportune moment; sucking helium from the globe and squeaking out the second verse; and referring repeatedly to 'chivers' without any word of explanation. Sebastien Tellier's 'Divine' was partly a send-up (I think), partly some kind of art installation, yet with a great Euro-tune at its core. It still goes down as one of my all-time ten favourite Eurovision Song Contest performances, though I still don't know exactly what point the superb Sebastien was trying to get across or what he was trying to achieve. Nor do I much care.

Because it's the ones that best defy definition, elude logic and confound comprehension that, for my money, invariably make the very best Eurovision novelty entries of all.

Postcard: Saturday 4th May 1985

It could have been me. Honestly. It really could have been me. Putting aside questions of luck and talent, I could have had my moment in the sun.

Many worse songs have been entered into the Eurovision Song Contest. There's always room for the odd lightweight or makeweight to slip like the Scarlet Pimpernel through the cordon and make it to the scaffold for ritual execution before the baying eyes of millions. If quality were a prerequisite for having your song selected for Eurovision, the Grand Final would generally be a head-to-head, two-person affair more akin to the World Chess Championship than to a breathless mile-long dash around the track, elbows flying, trying to fight your way to the front of a whole pack of non-elite athletes and then dip for the line just ahead of them.

That was pretty much the chilling and misplaced logic when I submitted a song for Austria ('*nul points*' no-hopers in 1984 and therefore, I assumed, pretty keen on receiving an entry for 1985 from the land of the Beatles and the Wombles). Yes, this was the fundamental basis of what passed for my reasoning as I sought to fly the red-white-and-red-again flag at the contest in Gothenburg. Did you get that? GOTHENBURG! IN SWEDEN! What clearer proof did I need that the prophecy of renowned sixteenth-century mystic Nostradamus was actually coming true – the prophecy where he said, just after predicting the Great Fire of London and Zayn Malik's departure from One Direction:

"And the one who is nearly Larry, but not quite, shall maketh music about trite things with a partially tuned guitar and this shall secure favour with the mountain men, who shall send the one who is nearly Larry, but not quite, to the icy northern land of the silver-booted blonde lady with the blue hat who turned his head when he was but an impressionable boy and saw her singing on the telly. And he shall wipeth the floor with the lot of them that do standeth in opposition against him."

Quite a visionary was our Nostradamus, foreseeing the invention of the television and, even more impressively, predicting an all-conquering trip to the land of ABBA for me and my trite song that I'd written for Austria. But there again, I hear you ask, what of his other prophecy – the one where he said:

"And a mighty voice shall speaketh unto him and it shall say: 'Listen, man who is nearly Larry, but not quite – you'll need a significantly better song than that, you prune. For is it not obvious that you are too delusional, even for the Eurovision Song Contest?'"

That's a stinging criticism, isn't it? Being told you're too delusional for Eurovision – that's like being told you're too tall for basketball or too damp for swimming.

Sadly, my capacity to blend big dreams with bum notes meant my song wouldn't end up competing in the thirtieth Eurovision Song Contest, to be held on the fourth of May 1985 in Gothenburg's mighty Scandinavium arena. No, I'd have to watch the fun unfold, as usual, on the TV – and that included the pre-song postcards which, for the first time ever, focused on the songwriters, as if to rub salt into my self-inflicted wound. Yes, it could have been me goofing around for the camera. But it wasn't. Here was May the Fourth and it would, most definitely, NOT be with me.

*　*　*　*　*　*

When, in his famous experiment, Ivan Pavlov started a metronome and his dog started salivating because it knew this was a sign that food was coming, I wonder whether it crossed Pavlov's mind to swap the metronome with Charpentier's party piece and replace the dog with a Eurovision fan? For me, that piece of music triggers a classic conditioned response: higher pulse rate, dilation of pupils, slight clamminess of the hands, involuntary reflex to snatch any slice of Parma ham within arm's reach, plus an irresistible urge to place my right hand over my heart and gaze slightly upwards, national anthem style. And tonight sees precisely the same response as we get our first glimpse of Gothenburg.

It looks a bit misty, or maybe that's just the tears in my eyes triggered by the conviction that this really could have been MY Eurovision. In fact, it looks like a shot of sunrise in Sweden's second city. No-one seems to be up and about and even the huge cranes at the port stand silent – like my musical dreams. (Note to self – let it go.) Has the city been abandoned? It's like a scene from 'The Omega Man' starring Charlton Heston – and I'm not talking about a film to do with a guy keen on fish-oil supplements.

Ah, at last we're homing in on the Scandinavium. And here's Lill Lindfors who'll be piloting us through the rapids this evening. She represented Sweden superbly at the 1966 contest and on this occasion she looks like she may have turned up in her PJs and dressing gown, so perhaps she's trying to tell us this could be a long evening. And Lill's breaking the mould by singing to us – a samba-y thing heavy on handclaps and tenor sax, and spinning some thesis about music and bricks. Indeed, no doubt someone here, at some point in the evening, will be dropping one or two of those as they flail about in the quest to deliver some quality light entertainment. Lill lobs in a Cleo Laine-style scat while the snake-hipped sax man, who may well be Eddie Shoestring, makes the very most of the primetime exposure.

Right, we're seven minutes in and there's no sign of a contestant yet. In fact, Lill informs us, there'll be nineteen contestants tonight. And they'll be backed by the house orchestra who are ensconced up on the left-hand part of what's actually a pretty vast stage and, conductor-wise, they'll be in the safe hands of what looks like one of the Buggles. Lys Assia, who won the first-ever Eurovision for

Switzerland back in 1956 apparently, pops up in the crowd to take a bow and Lill then informs us that tonight it's the songwriters who'll be in the spotlight. (Don't, Lill. This is killing me.) Indeed, there are all tonight's composers and lyricists, gathered together in a block in the audience like the prefects at a school play.

Ten minutes in and still not a Eurovision entry in sight. Isn't time elastic? What's the hurry? Lill still has a moment to say "hi" to her mum and to stretch things out a bit longer in order to inform us that Australia are watching along with six hundred million others. But just when it seems as if even elastic time must be about to go 'ping' and, if not snap entirely, at least be unsuitable to tie mittens together for the foreseeable future, we're finally, FINALLY ready for entry number one.

It's from Ireland, although Lill seems to have a small French flag in her hand for some reason that may have something to do with the Common Agricultural Policy. Then we're treated to a clip of the Irish songwriter jogging round Gothenburg in a natty green tracksuit and looking out towards some boats. Back inside the arena, Maria Christian plots an unflustered path through 'Wait Until the Weekend Comes', unaware perhaps that it already has. But Maria maintains the intermittent Irish tradition of going for and hitting the Johnny Logan high note right at the end and the show's finally on the road.

After Finland's songwriters have dabbled with a bit of glass-blowing and metal-working, it's time to meet Sonja Lumme and her backing singers. Well, it's time to meet the backs of their heads, anyway, as they're opting for the old start-with-your-back-to-the-camera routine. Always risky, of course, in case the audience and indeed the cameras aren't there anymore when you turn round. And in fact we miss the big turn-round moment for an essential shot of the back of Lill's head. Interestingly, Lill's staying on her stool up there on stage during all the entries tonight, just metres from the singers, perhaps in case she needs to apply emergency first aid or provide some counselling. Finland's song is actually a pretty decent slab of '80s pop, as it happens, featuring quintuple handclap volleys that ring out like rifle shots from the hands of the backing singers. And isn't it extraordinary how so much of people's hair spent so much of the 1980s pointing up or pointing out? If all inventions are the children of necessity, how come anyone came up with hair mousse? The song ends and a man in the crowd takes a photo – possibly for his upcoming Bad Hair Day exhibition.

After meeting some plants and sniffing one of them in a hothouse, singer-songwriter Lia Vissi from Cyprus is the next to take her place on a set that's reminiscent of the inside of a municipal leisure centre and includes what looks like a giant spacehopper. Eschewing the Finns' approach in favour of the old walk-on-from-the-back routine, Lia cranks through her ballad with just a man at a white piano for close company before we're treated to something very odd indeed.

After their songwriters have been shown meeting at a ferry terminal (ah – the glamour of the music business), Denmark's representatives Hot Eyes kick off their entry 'Sku' du Spørg' Fra No'en' ('What Business Is It of Yours?') with two shoulder-padded women and a shoulder-padded man with their backs to camera. (Finland have already beaten you to that one, I'm afraid.) But then a very small girl runs on and hides behind the man's legs. Ah, I see. The adults are actually the backing singers. Maybe the child's won some kind of competition. OK, we've finally found the lead singer who spins round to reveal much bigger shoulder pads. It's presumably a pecking order thing.

But hang on! Now the little girl's joined in with the chorus and is nicking clothing from the backing singers before running across the stage and starting to play dressing-up with her contraband. And now someone else has run on the stage and started to join in with the chorus as well. Are they acting out a reverse-custody battle? "You keep her." "No, you keep her – you're to blame for her kleptomania anyway…" And by the end of the song the 'couple' and their 'daughter' are warbling away side by side like the end of a bad 1970s US sitcom. I'm sure all of this sounded like a bloody good idea when someone outlined it at a meeting and drew pictures on a flipchart with a blue marker pen. And I'll bet someone uttered those fateful words: "trust me, it'll work…"

Another postcard, another boat. And then it's into Spain's Big Ballad. Apparently, the party's over but the singer Paloma isn't going anywhere just yet as she combines Shirley Bassey-esque big hand and arm gestures with 'Dynasty'-style big sparkly fashion. Paloma's certainly giving her Big Ballad the Big Belt, even with Lill sitting there at point-blank range. I wonder if she slipped some earplugs into her handbag?

Another postcard, another bloomin' boat. The conductor of the French entry has left his top button undone behind his tie, which I'm taking as a kind of statement of intent. Singer Roger Bens, meanwhile, has gone for a big baggy suit and as the song picks up a bit of pace in the chorus, he emits regular shouts of "femme!" which of course sounds like "fam!" and makes me want to shout back "I wanna live forever!" And after the orchestra have let out a bit of their inner Vivaldi, Roger extends his hand towards the camera apparently in a desperate plea for the object of his attentions to dance, and we're left to deduce that the answer which came back was "sur votre bicyclette".

Lill's doing a fine job, introducing the acts perched there on her stool like she's trialling a new format for a current affairs magazine show. And now she's brandishing a little Turkish flag as she summarises the main points of the news regarding Turkey's MFÖ and their song 'Didai Didai Dai', which is possibly just a strange nickname for a Welshman. Heads down and obscured by hats, the trio (presumably M, F and Ö) slowly pace towards their mikes and look just a little like master bakers in their white jackets, white trousers and white trilbies. It's all very happy and clappy and even Lill's standing up now. And as a bonus there are synthesised handclaps that no self-respecting mid-'80s crowd-pleaser should be without. Highly enjoyable.

Belgium's ballad 'Laat Me Nu Gaan' doesn't make much of an impact, but at least the songwriters got the chance to visit an amusement park. The writers of Portugal's ballad, meanwhile, seem to be waiting for a ferry and then they pick up some valuable skills in fishing net preparation which will presumably help them find a good hook. (That's a proper musical joke, by the way.) Singer Adelaide's silver-tassel epaulettes and silver-tassel skirt appear to be drawing comment from her backing singers, who seem to be whispering about something, and maybe she's taken mortal offence as she sinks to the floor at the end of the performance, crossing her legs, and the camera leaves her sixty percent of the way towards adopting the foetal position. I know how she feels. That's how Eurovision gets you sometimes. (Further note to self: I SAID LEAVE IT!)

OK, here are tonight's bookies' favourites, a label that's generally an utter kiss of death, of course. It's Wind from Germany with 'Für Alle' ('For Everyone'). Lill reads out the customary notes from a mini national flag and then on comes conductor Reiner Pietsch, who looks like he's auditioning for a role in 'Anchor Man'. His frilly-fronted peach shirt perfectly complements the shades and the big droopy 'tache, and I think our quest for the definitive Eurovision conductor may at long, long last finally be over. Then, as the song makes its move, it dawns on me. Finger clicks! That's where I went wrong with my entry! I remembered the synthesised handclaps but I forgot the finger clicks! This six-piece band don't, though, as they tout their pleasant brand of synth pop. (Toto Cutugno will, however. take clicking digits up another notch in five years' time.)

One of the singers is straight out of the Nena catalogue, which can only be categorised as a welcome development, and this is all good, solid stuff. There's even a bit of modulation and one of the keyboard players throws in a nice little soprano wail near the end. Big in the hall, that one.

Now, what's this? Here's a blast from the past. Izhar Cohen's back, representing Israel seven years after his famous Eurovision triumph in Paris. He seems to have ditched Alpha Beta (which always sounded like spaghetti hoops to me anyway) but on the other hand he's brought a conductor with proper mid-'80s rolled-up jacket sleeves. Well, I say they're rolled-up but maybe they're cut off – you know, like those cut-off denims that park footballers wore when they couldn't be bothered to shell out for a pair of Kevin Keegan-style crotch-hugging shorts. He kisses Lill's hand, which will teach her for not vacating the stage, and then we're treated to the sight of five party people with their backs to camera. A blur of guys in red, blue and yellow, complemented by two girls in short turquoise and pink dresses, they've got a definite Bucks Fizz-plus air about them and then Izhar, resplendent in white and with Kevin Keegan-esque barnet, comes steaming down the stairs at the back and we're headlong into 'Olé Olé'. Yelps, whoops, good energy, plenty of synthesised handclaps – all good fun and the guy in red with the headband seems happier than anyone has any right to be on a public stage. The overall effect isn't so much 'Kids from Fame' as 'Kids from Fizz', which is far from being a bad thing, but overall I feel this one may just come up short.

Talking of returning favourites, here are Italy's 1976 vintage Al and Romina to have another pop at the title. At first, the preview postcard looks like it may have latched onto a couple of guys from Special Branch, but it's actually the songwriters of 'Magic Oh Magic'. And Lill seems to be reading from notes printed on the French flag again, as she did for Ireland's song. No, I get it now – the printer's obviously got a problem with greens! It's printing them too dark. Slightly relieving to know I'm not the only person with a crap printer. I'll bet they've had a few problems with paper jams too. Al and Romina, meanwhile, are certainly sticking to the tried and tested here, as they take turns to walk to centre stage. After a slightly shaky start, with viewers hopefully distracted by Romina's voluminous sparkly dress, it's clear this is a much stronger song than their effort nine years ago and there are very, very few songs in the whole of creation that won't benefit significantly from including a 'wo-oh-oh' bit near the end.

Now I'm sufficiently delusional to still be completely confident, at this point in proceedings, that my song would have kept its head well above water tonight. I might have been tempted to pass over the chance of a chopper trip to an oil rig, to be truthful, but the Norwegian songwriter is clearly made of much sterner stuff than me. Personally, a helicopter would have been no place for someone with a morbid fear of flying and who had so much more to give to the world from a musical perspective. Rolf Løvland, on the other hand, is even sanguine enough to fiddle with some knobs on the oil rig's control panel. Presumably Red Adair has been put on standby but can't appear in the postcard as he hasn't written a Eurovision entry. Not even 'Pet'r Oil'.

But oil price shocks are probably the least of Norway's worries tonight as they continue their thankless battle against the grossly unfair but pretty deep-seated perception that, as 'nul points' specialists, they're one of Eurovision's primary joke countries. Some of us rail against that orthodoxy – and are still considering setting up a fan club specifically for 1968's outrageously underrated masterpiece, Odd Børre's 'Stress'. If you haven't heard of it, all I can say is that it's what the internet's for.

The conductor's got rolled-up sleeves and a turned-up collar, so that's a decent start anyway. And now here come Bobbysocks!, rushing on from the back and egged on by their backing singers who look as though they may have a sweepstake on which of the two girls in purple spangly jackets will get to the front first. Just for the record, it was the girl without gloves. The girl with gloves was presumably halfway through checking the oil level in her car when she got called to the stage. But I'm glad they made it as 'La Det Swinge' ('Let It Swing') certainly has plenty of jump and jive about it, fuelled by a big, swingin' blast of brass. Can they find a chorus, though? Come on, girls! Shock the world! YES! What a refrain! Hi-ho, it's to the upper reaches of the scoreboard you go, surely. The girls throw their hands out for the big finish and get a BIG reception. There's plenty of support for Norway here tonight, and not just because Bobbysocks! are fifty percent Norwegian and fifty percent Norwegian-Swedish (so twenty-five percent Swedish basically, according to my pocket calculator, now that I've wiped the word 'GOOLIES' off it).

Follow that. Well, that's what the UK's Vikki needs to do now with 'Love Is'. But they've taken her and her fellow songwriter to a stately home with massive windows and big balconies so that's surely set her up for a decent performance tonight. Hopefully that white chair wasn't purloined from the property in question. Vikki possibly needs the chair in order to help support her splendid hairdo, which is a masterpiece of civil engineering and something that the Swedes, kings of suspension bridges, are bound to admire. A nice mid-paced song, nicely delivered – but there was definitely a big space there just yearning for some synthesised handclaps. I can spot that sort of thing. And the shots of the crowd right at the end seem to indicate that Her Majesty's loyal press corps quite enjoyed it – or maybe they're just enjoying a weekend away from Thatcher's Britain (a.k.a. Britain, of course, if you voted Conservative).

The Swiss songwriters are taken to a camera factory and appear to be asking the woman who's showing them round a variety of questions, presumably along the lines of "HOW long to get them developed?" I'm not picturing success when I hear the song 'Piano

Piano', though, and I'm more enthused by the prospect of sampling what the host nation have got in store for us. Sweden are defending their title with the song 'Bra Vibrationer', which sounds a lot less interesting in Swedish than it looks in English. It actually means 'Good Vibrations' and will be sung by Kikki Danielsson – after we've seen the songwriters visit a fish market, sample some prawns and generally look for inspiration on how to make their entry more turbot-charged. (That's another proper joke, incidentally.) Then it's all down to Kikki and her pink jacket, aided by two mime-style dancers with an exemplary work rate. A decent up-tempo song predictably receives a rapturous home reception.

Right. Now this may hurt. I don't want you to panic. Just tell me if it gets too painful. And don't start crying. Again. No, I'm not quoting my dentist. In fact, I'm talking to myself and preparing for the Austrian entry. To misquote a famous movie, I might have been that contender. I certainly could have sat on the end beside the songwriters and helped them hoover up the cakes in that Viennese-style café. Holding a mini red-white-and-red-again flag, Lill informs us that 'Kinder Dieser Welt' will be sung by Gary Lux. And Gary's got a happy five-piece band with him as we get a count-in and he wanders round to his piano and clicks his mike into place before launching into his instantly catchy, instantly clearly-better-than-mine song. Right. That's enough brutal honesty for one lifetime. It's much more fun being delusional. I wonder which country might be desperate for an entry next year?

Let's move on. In every sense.

'Dschinghis Khan'. 'Papa Pingouin'. 'Ein Bisschen Frieden'. 'Theater'. 'Sing Sang Song'. Just five of the Eurovision songs that German songwriter Ralph Siegel has had a hand in and Ralph's part of the team behind tonight's Luxembourg entry too. I wonder if Ralph started off by unsuccessfully submitting a song for Austria? I'd like to think so – or need to believe it, if you really do prefer that brutal

200

honesty thing. Three male-female pairs are singing 'Children, Kinder, Enfants' ('Children, Children, Children', but it loses some of the impact just in English, doesn't it?) and they're all dressed completely in white. So presumably anyone visiting their dressing-room beforehand with a bottle of tomato ketchup or a tin of blue paint wouldn't have been very welcome. There's actually quite a lot going on in the song, in terms of counter-melodies and complexity. It's the sort of song you need a kind of aerial view of to see what goes where and how it all fits together. Perhaps Rolf Løvland could go up in Red Adair's helicopter and radio back that information for me.

Last and not inconceivably least, it's Greece and they're using the same job-share conductor as Cyprus. It's an unremarkable ballad called 'Miazoume' ('We Are Alike'), although credit where it's due – singer Takis Biniaris does a great job when you take into account the fact that he's got to contend with Lill sitting there just a matter of metres away from him, like a judge on 'Eurovision's Got Talent'.

So the songs are over. Lill's got a red rose from somewhere and goes for a short walk to introduce tonight's interval act, acoustic guitar duo Guitars Unlimited, who run through a medley of jazzy, folky and Latino-style tunes while we're treated to some shots of the sea, the sky and a boat. And a couple more boats. Oh and that's another boat. Now it's fields, flowers and trees. Frankly, I preferred the boats.

*   *   *   *   *   *

OK, Lill's back now and HER SKIRT HAS SNAGGED ON SOMETHING AND BEEN RIPPED OFF! No, I'm not having one of 'my' dreams. It really has! Gasps of shock and astonishment! But no, no – we've all been expertly 'had', as Lill instantly releases something on her shoulders and her top turns into a full-length white dress. Very neat. I think I'm relieved. And Lill now heads for the chat show part of the set where she sits down with what looks like the wine list, quite close to a very large bubble. We get a sight of the big electronic scoreboard and meet tonight's Voting Scrutineer Frank Naef, Clifford Brown having now passed into the esteemed vaults of Eurovision folklore.

As I won't be there to pick up the trophy on this occasion, let's see who's going to get lucky instead, shall we? Ireland award the first point of the evening to Cyprus. The UK get five but the big wads go to Sweden with ten and – yes – NORWAY with twelve. Mild pandemonium breaks out as Eurovision's 'poor relations' actually get a taste of what it's like to sit on top of the pile. But Finland's twelve for Sweden propels the hosts above them before Cyprus perform the same service for Germany, who now lead the field, with Sweden second and Norway and Italy equal third. And as more juries declare (including Denmark, whose spokesman sounds a bit gloomy, so he clearly caught sight of his country's song earlier) Germany maintain that position and open up a healthy lead that gives them a game in hand over their closest rivals, which now also include Israel (no doubt giving red-headband man cause to spread his smile even wider, if that were possible). The UK haul themselves into contention too, but now it's Germany's to lose – and now it's Germany to vote.

Five for the UK, six for Denmark, seven for Israel, eight for Sweden, ten for Austria and twelve for Norway. Colossal cheers. But despite having voted and with all their key rivals yet to do so (and therefore potentially losing ground because they can't vote for their own songs), Germany still have a lead of thirteen over Sweden while Norway are just behind Italy, in equal fourth with the UK. But another twelve for Norway, this time from Israel, brings them into second place on their own and, now only eleven points behind, they're within touching distance of the Germans.

But it's all about to get phenomenally tight and by the time Italy, Norway and the UK have delivered their verdicts, it's Germany on eighty-seven, Sweden on eighty-six and Norway on eighty-five. Then, perhaps, we have a turning point as Switzerland give Germany a big round zero, allowing both Sweden and Norway to sneak past them. And Sweden's own votes enable Norway to bound back to the top with another dollop of *douze points*, while Germany sneak back into second. There are just three juries left to declare.

Here's Austria. Will they reciprocate and send a major points consignment up the Danube to tilt things back Germany's way? Will they get the hump with those who didn't vote for them last year? This Eurovision voting business really can get like those tedious tit-for-tat expulsions of embassy staff that seem to endlessly amuse governments all over the world. Just four points for Sweden, putting them on ninety-eight. It's ten for Ireland, so where's the big twelve going? Either Germany or Norway are going to miss out completely. And IT'S NORWAY WHO GET IT! And that puts them seventeen clear. In the space of just two juries they've broken free – and now the Cinderellas of Eurovision are on the verge of flicking the bird at all the scoffers, mockers, jeerers, jibers, taunters, teasers, sneerers and snotty little so-and-sos who've delighted in their string of reverses down the years.

Keep that breath bated. Luxembourg have the power. And seven points for Norway is all that they needed. It's decided. It's all over. Cinderella has not only gone to the ball. She's kicked the door in, downed the Moët & Chandon, grabbed a huge handful of vol-au-vents, sacked the orchestra and stuck 'Dancing Queen' on the CD player at top blast. Even Greece's slightly offbeat set of votes – none for Germany, none for Sweden, one for Norway – can't change a thing, though their eight for Cyprus should ensure only minimal tit-for-tat expulsions are needed between those two countries.

Well, well, well. It's all flowers and champagne in the green room. Is it someone's wedding anniversary? Lill announces the winners and here come Herreys (in conventional footwear this year) to make the presentation, while Lill reminds us not just of how often in the past Norway have finished last but also of the Swedish blood that courses through the veins of half of Bobbysocks! – and foreshadowing the Rent-a-Swede years of Eurovision which lie ahead. Lill even allows herself the liberty of a discreet bop during the reprise and hopefully there won't be any unscheduled repeat of the skirt business.

Bobbysocks!, meanwhile, have no need to run on stage this time as they're already there. The girls slip in an English chorus just before the powerhouse ending, there's more big hugs to be had and then Lill signs off and signs out. As for me, having heard 'La Det Swinge' not once but twice now, I'm left with the dawning, crushing realisation that, after all, in terms of lifting the 1985 Eurovision trophy, well – it absolutely and categorically really COULDN'T have been me.

I think we can call that 'closure'.

Confounding the Critics

Can I have a private word? It's a bit delicate. You see, I've got a dreadful confession to make. The thing is, I've never actually physically been to the Eurovision Song Contest. I've never, ever attended in person. There's no denying that people are often very, very surprised when I cry out: "I'm sorry – I've never been to Eurovision!" Especially when we're in a lift together and they're complete strangers. Though just once, I suppose, I'd like one of them to shout back: "NEITHER HAVE I!"

I blame science. Science has achieved some very, very clever things. It's pinpointed the 'God' particle. It's untangled the mysteries of the human genome. It's done stuff with stem cells that I don't really understand. It's even come up with popping candy. But it's yet to find a way of enabling me to be in two places at the same time. You see, I NEED to be in front of a TV for Eurovision. That's how it's always been. Year in, year out, for decades. It's a tradition thing. In the same way that a family's Christmas traditions end up exerting a kind of tyranny over them, handcuffing them to doing the same things at the same times with the same people year after year after year, so it is with me and Eurovision. Only in a good way. It's how the world has to work, in order for it to work at all.

More than that, if I break the magic circle that's brought me this far on my Eurovision odyssey, perhaps the spell will be broken. Perhaps some of the magic will be dissipated. What if I went to Eurovision and I didn't enjoy it quite as much as I should? What if my seat only offered me a restricted view, behind a concrete pillar or a tall Swede? What if I had a bad seat with bad acoustics or someone behind me shouting down my ear (an off-duty Czech DJ, for instance)? What if one of those big inflatable Israeli hammers caught me on the back of the head or, worse still, obscured Mr Lordi just at the moment he was extending his serpent wings? Or at precisely the point when Lill Lindfors lost her skirt? If any of this were to happen, might I just end up getting a bit irritated? Might I actually experience what would previously have counted as the unthinkable: negative thoughts about Eurovision? Just imagine. I'd have to write another book about it – and none of us really want that.

It's a bit like a football supporter and their lucky pants. Wear the pants and their team's guaranteed to win. Get their wash cycle just a day out of sync and be forced to wear alternative, unlucky or even luck-neutral pants and the ramifications are almost impossible to comprehend – perhaps a centre-back losing possession just outside his own penalty area and watching in horror as the opposition's winger curls the ball into the top left-hand corner for a last-minute winner. In the same way, I know I'd better not meddle with the laws of time and space where Eurovision's concerned. I know exactly what I need to do and where I need to be on Eurovision Night and, indeed, throughout the whole of Eurovision Week. If I get it wrong, it could be disastrous. EVERYONE'S Eurovision could be in danger. Mine, yours, Graham Norton's.

And if Eurovision should be affected adversely by me breaking my side of the cosmic bargain, who would actually win? I'll tell you. The people who hate Eurovision, that's who. The Eurovision-phobes. The Eurovision deniers. The cynics and the critics who spare no effort or opportunity to tell us what's wrong with the entire Eurovision bandwagon and why we'd all be better off without it. In short, the people we can never, ever allow to win!

You don't get to my time of life without realising that, in this perplexing world of ours, there are an awful lot of people who talk an awful lot of complete cobblers. And a decent proportion of that sum total of scrotal nonsense is talked about the Eurovision Song Contest. Let's just take three examples and call these people out and address them directly:

It's All Got So Predictable: No it hasn't. Did you foresee the human hamster wheel in 2014? And how can you say it's obvious who's going to win when, between 2001 and 2014, we saw fourteen contests won by fourteen different countries – from east and west, from north and south, and with the then Big Four even delivering a winner in 2010. Blimey, even Portugal won in 2017!

It's All About Political and Neighbourly Voting: Utter tosh. Voting for the next-door country (with which your country has probably spent, at a conservative estimate, nine hundred of the past thousand years competing, arguing and warring) as a result of some inexplicable warm glow that comes over you once a year on Eurovision Night is a little fanciful, don't you think? The voting patterns you spend so much time complaining about (and whose impact is often overstated anyway) are actually largely the result of ex-pats or minorities voting for the motherland, or culturally similar people from the same region donating votes because they like similar music. Forget the conspiracy theories. Human incompetence makes conspiracies incredibly hard to pull off once, let alone year after year. Just ask Guy Fawkes. Oh. You can't. Which is exactly the point.

It Used to Be Much Better in the Old Days: Palpable cobblers. Would more than a tiny fraction of the people who make this particular claim genuinely rather watch, say, the whole of the 1989 contest than the whole of the 2014 contest? Back in the twentieth century, not everyone sounded like ABBA. It's better now than it's ever been. It's got better songs, better crowds, better production values, better camerawork, better everything. Was there ever a better show than 2016's in Sweden? And WHAT a finish! As Ukraine pipped Australia and Russia with literally the last roll of the metaphorical dice, I think the whole of Europe (and beyond) was left in urgent need of collective blood-pressure medication.

Let's face it, Eurovision has been confounding its critics ever since it began, when Lys Assia won in 1956, by all accounts. Sixty-one years on, its strength is still growing. Cynics never like to be proved wrong and the contest's rude health continues to see them marooned on the wrong side of history, the wrong side of the argument and the wrong side of the Eurovision tracks. The only thing we can say for certain is that Eurovision will never stand still. Nor should it. And I'll confidently predict that, even in the year 2030, it'll still be far and away the best, most enthralling, most entertaining night of the year.

So put your mind at rest. That's the way it's going to stay.

Just as long as I don't actually go and watch it.

Postcard: Monday 13ᵗʰ May 2030

We're thirty years into the third millennium and so many things in the world change these days that it's nice to have SOMETHING you can rely on. What with the announcement that Antarctica will be hosting the 2034 soccer World Cup and the recent news from the Luyten's star system that they enjoyed the pictures of Lordi's Eurovision victory which finally reached them but didn't realise some earthlings looked like that, it's somehow reassuring to get back to normal and enjoy a typical Eurovision week. And of course we've got a particular reason to celebrate this year, as we mark the seventy-fifth contest in the show's loud and proud history, dating all the way back to 1956 when, I'm told, Lys Assia won it for Switzerland.

So it's Monday and that can only mean one thing. Yes, that's right – it's the first instalment in the contest's Group Stages and the crowd here in Poland are going absolutely nuts. And when I say Poland, I don't mean Poland. No, I mean the village of Poland on Christmas Island, part of the Pacific Republic of Kiribati and just down the road from the village of London and the ruins of the village of Paris. (Check a map if you don't believe me.) And the Minidome is absolutely jam-packed with Eurovision fans who've gathered together to see nine countries, six transnational regions and twenty-three breakaway republics battle it out for the first ten places available in Saturday's fifty-six-strong Grand Final.

There's absolutely no sign of the locals' ardour for the contest being diminished, despite this being the fourth year in a row that the Eurovision circus has come to town following Kiribati's historic fourth successive victory last year with 'Heroes and Phoenixes'. That song, of course, secured a record score from the telepathicvoting public – even if it didn't fare quite so well with the millions of jury nodes activated inside the contest's very own proprietary hyper-secure transultracomputer 'Con-cheater', which (if you remember) showed a significant preference for the somewhat retro Swedish entry 'Water-Loo, Water-Ley'.

The two hot favourites tonight are Italy with their entry 'Still Insieme (Well, Most of Us): 2032' and Ireland's 'Rock 'n' Roll Great-Grandkids' but you certainly couldn't write off Mexico's chances, or those of the representatives of the manned Mars base whose entry 'Hello from Latvia' has been gathering some very positive reviews. And we're also anticipating an intriguing nostalgia spot during tonight's voting interval, which I'm told will poke affectionate fun at the crazy old ways of Eurovision back in 2017 when people had to vote with things called smartphones and all the contestants actually had to turn up in person at the venue to perform their songs. Stone Age or what!

Thank heavens for transportable 5-D robo-holograms! How did the Eurovision Song Contest ever manage without them? And thank heavens, too, that the widely mooted idea of inviting the Luyten's star system to cast votes wasn't finally given the green light, as that would have delayed the announcement of the result by an estimated twenty-four and a half years – just a shade longer than the normal voting procedure.

So! Let the show begin! And let me take this opportunity to wish each and every one of you a very, very, <u>VERY</u> Merry Eurovision!

Voting: Decision Time

Year: 1956
Location: Lugano, Switzerland
Winner: Lys Assia (Switzerland), 'Refrain'
UK entry: None
Garry's Gold Medal: Fud Leclerc (Belgium), 'Messieurs les Noyés de la Seine'

Year: 1957
Location: Frankfurt, Germany
Winner: Corry Brokken (the Netherlands), 'Net Als Toen'
UK entry: Patricia Bredin, 'All' (7th)
Garry's Gold Medal: Bob Martin (Austria), 'Wohin, Kleines Pony?'

Year: 1958
Location: Hilversum, the Netherlands
Winner: André Claveau (France), 'Dors, Mon Amour'
UK entry: None
Garry's Gold Medal: Margot Hielscher (Germany), 'Für Zwei Groschen Musik'

Year: 1959
Location: Cannes, France
Winner: Teddy Scholten (the Netherlands), ''n Beetje'
UK entry: Pearl Carr & Teddy Johnson, 'Sing, Little Birdie' (2nd)
Garry's Gold Medal: Birthe Wilke (Denmark), 'Uh, Jeg Ville Ønske Jeg Var Dig'

Year: 1960
Location: London, the UK
Winner: Jacqueline Boyer (France), 'Tom Pillibi'

UK entry: Bryan Johnson, 'Looking High, High, High' (2nd)
Garry's Gold Medal: Nora Brockstedt (Norway), 'Voi Voi'

Year: 1961

Location: Cannes, France
Winner: Jean-Claude Pascal (Luxembourg), 'Nous les Amoureux'
UK entry: The Allisons, 'Are You Sure?' (2nd)
Garry's Gold Medal: Greetje Kauffeld (the Netherlands), 'Wat een Dag'

Year: 1962

Location: Luxembourg City, Luxembourg
Winner: Isabelle Aubret (France), 'Un Premier Amour'
UK entry: Ronnie Carroll, 'Ring-a-Ding Girl' (equal 4th)
Garry's Gold Medal: Conny Froboess (Germany), 'Zwei Kleiner Italiener'

Year: 1963

Location: London, the UK
Winner: Grethe & Jørgen Ingmann (Denmark), 'Dansevise'
UK entry: Ronnie Carroll, 'Say Wonderful Things' (4th)
Garry's Gold Medal: Heidi Brühl (Germany), 'Marcel'

Year: 1964

Location: Copenhagen, Denmark
Winner: Gigliola Cinquetti (Italy), 'Non Ho l'Età'
UK entry: Matt Monro, 'I Love the Little Things' (2nd)
Garry's Gold Medal: Anneke Grönloh (the Netherlands), 'Jij Bent Mijn Leven'

Year: 1965

Location: Naples, Italy
Winner: France Gall (Luxembourg), 'Poupée de Cire, Poupée de Son'

UK entry: Kathy Kirby, 'I Belong' (2nd)
Garry's Gold Medal: Luxembourg

Year: 1966
Location: Luxembourg City, Luxembourg
Winner: Udo Jürgens (Austria), 'Merci, Chérie'
UK entry: Kenneth McKellar, 'A Man Without Love' (9th)
Garry's Gold Medal: Åse Kleveland (Norway), 'Intet er Nytt under Solen'

Year: 1967
Location: Vienna, Austria
Winner: Sandie Shaw (the UK), 'Puppet on a String'
Garry's Gold Medal: Vicky Leandros (Luxembourg), 'L'Amour est Bleu'

Year: 1968
Location: London, the UK
Winner: Massiel (Spain), 'La, La, La'
UK entry: Cliff Richard, 'Congratulations' (2nd)
Garry's Gold Medal: Odd Børre (Norway), 'Stress'

Year: 1969
Location: Madrid, Spain
Joint Winners: Salomé (Spain), 'Vivo Cantando'; Lulu (the UK), 'Boom Bang-a-Bang'; Lenny Kuhr (the Netherlands), 'De Troubadour'; Frida Boccara (France), 'Un Jour, Un Enfant'
Garry's Gold Medal: Tommy Körberg (Sweden), 'Judy, Min Vän'

Year: 1970
Location: Amsterdam, the Netherlands
Winner: Dana (Ireland), 'All Kinds of Everything'
UK entry: Mary Hopkin, 'Knock Knock (Who's There?)' (2nd)

Garry's Gold Medal: Katja Ebstein (Germany), 'Wunder Gibt Es Immer Wieder'

Year: 1971
Location: Dublin, Ireland
Winner: Séverine (Monaco), 'Un Banc, Un Arbre, Une Rue'
UK entry: Clodagh Rodgers, 'Jack in the Box' (4th)
Garry's Gold Medal: Monaco

Year: 1972
Location: Edinburgh, the UK
Winner: Vicky Leandros (Luxembourg), 'Après Toi'
UK entry: The New Seekers, 'Beg, Steal or Borrow' (2nd)
Garry's Gold Medal: The Milestones (Austria), 'Falter im Wind'

Year: 1973
Location: Luxembourg City, Luxembourg
Winner: Anne-Marie David (Luxembourg), 'Tu te Reconnaîtras'
UK entry: Cliff Richard, 'Power to All Our Friends' (3rd)
Garry's Gold Medal: Luxembourg

Year: 1974
Location: Brighton, the UK
Winner: ABBA (Sweden), 'Waterloo'
UK entry: Olivia Newton-John, 'Long Live Love' (equal 4th)
Garry's Gold Medal: Sweden

Year: 1975
Location: Stockholm, Sweden
Winner: Teach-In (the Netherlands), 'Ding Dinge Dong'
UK entry: The Shadows, 'Let Me Be the One' (2nd)
Garry's Gold Medal: Simone Drexel (Switzerland), 'Mikado'

Year: 1976
Location: The Hague, the Netherlands
Winner: Brotherhood of Man (the UK), 'Save Your Kisses for Me'
Garry's Gold Medal: Freddie & the Friends (Finland), 'Pump-Pump'

Year: 1977
Location: London, the UK
Winner: Marie Myriam (France), 'L'Oiseau et l'Enfant'
UK entry: Lynsey de Paul & Mike Moran, 'Rock Bottom' (2nd)
Garry's Gold Medal: Silver Convention (Germany), 'Telegram'

Year: 1978
Location: Paris, France
Winner: Izhar Cohen & Alpha Beta (Israel), 'A-Ba-Ni-Bi'
UK entry: Co-Co, 'The Bad Old Days' (11th)
Garry's Gold Medal: Springtime (Austria), 'Mrs Caroline Robinson'

Year: 1979
Location: Jerusalem, Israel
Winner: Gali Atari and Milk & Honey (Israel), 'Hallelujah'
UK entry: Black Lace, 'Mary Ann' (7th)
Garry's Gold Medal: Dschinghis Khan (Germany), 'Dschinghis Khan'

Year: 1980
Location: The Hague, the Netherlands
Winner: Johnny Logan (Ireland), 'What's Another Year?'
UK entry: Prima Donna, 'Love Enough for Two' (3rd)
Garry's Gold Medal: Telex (Belgium), 'Euro-Vision'

Year: 1981
Location: Dublin, Ireland
Winner: Bucks Fizz (the UK), 'Making Your Mind Up'
Garry's Gold Medal: Björn Skifs (Sweden), 'Fångad i en Dröm'

Year: 1982
Location: Harrogate, the UK
Winner: Nicole (Germany), 'Ein Bisschen Frieden'
UK entry: Bardo, 'One Step Further' (7th)
Garry's Gold Medal: Kojo (Finland), 'Nuku Pommiin'

Year: 1983
Location: Munich, Germany
Winner: Corinne Hermès (Luxembourg), 'Si la Vie est Cadeau'
UK entry: Sweet Dreams, 'I'm Never Giving Up' (6th)
Garry's Gold Medal: Daniel (Yugoslavia), 'Džuli'

Year: 1984
Location: Luxembourg City, Luxembourg
Winner: Herreys (Sweden), 'Diggi-Loo Diggi-Ley'
UK entry: Belle & the Devotions, 'Love Games' (7th)
Garry's Gold Medal: Linda Martin (Ireland), 'Terminal Three'

Year: 1985
Location: Gothenburg, Sweden
Winner: Bobbysocks! (Norway), 'La Det Swinge'
UK entry: Vikki, 'Love Is' (4th)
Garry's Gold Medal: Norway

Year: 1986
Location: Bergen, Norway
Winner: Sandra Kim (Belgium), 'J'Aime la Vie'
UK entry: Ryder, 'Runner in the Night' (7th)
Garry's Gold Medal: Frizzle Sizzle (the Netherlands), 'Alles Heeft Ritme'

Year: 1987
Location: Brussels, Belgium
Winner: Johnny Logan (Ireland), 'Hold Me Now'
UK entry: Rikki, 'Only the Light' (13th)
Garry's Gold Medal: Liliane Saint-Pierre (Belgium), 'Soldiers of Love'

Year: 1988
Location: Dublin, Ireland
Winner: Céline Dion (Switzerland), 'Ne Partez Pas Sans Moi'
UK entry: Scott Fitzgerald, 'Go' (2nd)
Garry's Gold Medal: Gerard Joling (the Netherlands), 'Shangri-La'

Year: 1989
Location: Lausanne, Switzerland
Winner: Riva (Yugoslavia), 'Rock Me'
UK entry: Live Report, 'Why Do I Always Get It Wrong?' (2nd)
Garry's Gold Medal: Da Vinci (Portugal), 'Conquistador'

Year: 1990
Location: Zagreb, Yugoslavia
Winner: Toto Cutugno (Italy), 'Insieme: 1992'
UK entry: Emma, 'Give a Little Love Back to the World' (6th)
Garry's Gold Medal: Italy

Year: 1991
Location: Rome, Italy
Winner: Carola (Sweden), 'Fångad av en Stormwind'
UK entry: Samantha Janus, 'A Message to Your Heart' (equal 10th)
Garry's Gold Medal: Baby Doll (Yugoslavia), 'Brazil'

Year: 1992
Location: Malmö, Sweden
Winner: Linda Martin (Ireland), 'Why Me?'

UK entry: Michael Ball, 'One Step out of Time' (2nd)
Garry's Gold Medal: Kali (France), 'Monté la Riviè'

Year: 1993
Location: Millstreet, Ireland
Winner: Niamh Kavanagh (Ireland), 'In Your Eyes'
UK entry: Sonia, 'Better the Devil You Know' (2nd)
Garry's Gold Medal: Münchener Freiheit (Germany), 'Viel zu Weit'

Year: 1994
Location: Dublin, Ireland
Winner: Harrington & McGettigan (Ireland), 'Rock 'n' Roll Kids'
UK entry: Frances Ruffelle, 'We Will Be Free' (10th)
Garry's Gold Medal: Mekado (Germany), 'Wir Geben 'ne Party'

Year: 1995
Location: Dublin, Ireland
Winner: Secret Garden (Norway), 'Nocturne'
UK entry: Love City Groove, 'Love City Groove' (equal 10th)
Garry's Gold Medal: Anabel Conde (Spain), 'Vuelve Conmigo'

Year: 1996
Location: Oslo, Norway
Winner: Eimear Quinn (Ireland), 'The Voice'
UK entry: Gina G, 'Ooh Aah...Just a Little Bit' (8th)
Garry's Gold Medal: the UK

Year: 1997
Location: Dublin, Ireland
Winner: Katrina & the Waves (the UK), 'Love Shine a Light'
Garry's Gold Medal: the UK

Year: 1998

Location: Birmingham, the UK

Winner: Dana International (Israel), 'Diva'

UK entry: Imaani, 'Where Are You?' (2nd)

Garry's Gold Medal: Guildo Horn (Germany), 'Guildo Hat Euch Lieb!'

Year: 1999

Location: Jerusalem, Israel

Winner: Charlotte Nilsson (Sweden), 'Take Me to Your Heaven'

UK entry: Precious, 'Say It Again' (equal 12th)

Garry's Gold Medal: Doris Dragović (Croatia), 'Marija Magdalena'

Year: 2000

Location: Stockholm, Sweden

Winner: The Olsen Brothers (Denmark), 'Fly on the Wings of Love'

UK entry: Nicki French, 'Don't Play that Song Again' (16th)

Garry's Gold Medal: Stefan Raab (Germany), 'Wadde Hadde Dudde Da?'

Year: 2001

Location: Copenhagen, Denmark

Winner: Tanel Padar & Dave Benton with 2XL (Estonia), 'Everybody'

UK entry: Lindsay Dracass, 'No Dream Impossible' (15th)

Garry's Gold Medal: Nino Pršeš (Bosnia-Herzegovina), 'Hano'

Year: 2002

Location: Tallinn, Estonia

Winner: Marie N (Latvia), 'I Wanna'

UK entry: Jessica Garlick, 'Come Back' (equal 3rd)

Garry's Gold Medal: Sahlene (Estonia), 'Runaway'

Year: 2003

Location: Riga, Latvia

Winner: Sertab Erener (Turkey), 'Everyway That I Can'
UK entry: Jemini, 'Cry Baby' (26th)
Garry's Gold Medal: Nicola (Romania), 'Don't Break My Heart'

Year: 2004
Location: Istanbul, Turkey
Winner: Ruslana (Ukraine), 'Wild Dances'
UK entry: James Fox, 'Hold On to Our Love' (16th)
Garry's Gold Medal: Blue Café (Poland), 'Love Song'

Year: 2005
Location: Kiev, Ukraine
Winner: Helena Paparizou (Greece), 'My Number One'
UK entry: Javine, 'Touch My Fire' (22nd)
Garry's Gold Medal: Glennis Grace (the Netherlands), 'My Impossible Dream'

Year: 2006
Location: Athens, Greece
Winner: Lordi (Finland), 'Hard Rock Hallelujah'
UK entry: Daz Sampson, 'Teenage Life' (19th)
Garry's Gold Medal: Kate Ryan (Belgium), 'Je t'Adore'

Year: 2007
Location: Helsinki, Finland
Winner: Marija Šerifović (Serbia), 'Molitva'
UK entry: Scooch, 'Flying the Flag (for You)' (equal 22nd)
Garry's Gold Medal: Verka Serduchka (Ukraine), 'Dancing Lasha Tumbai'

Year: 2008
Location: Belgrade, Serbia
Winner: Dima Bilan (Russia), 'Believe'

UK entry: Andy Abraham, 'Even If' (equal 23rd)
Garry's Gold Medal: Sebastien Tellier (France), 'Divine'

Year: 2009
Location: Moscow, Russia
Winner: Alexander Rybak (Norway), 'Fairytale'
UK entry: Jade Ewen, 'It's My Time' (5th)
Garry's Gold Medal: Svetlana Loboda (Ukraine), 'Be My Valentine!
(Anti-Crisis Girl)'

Year: 2010
Location: Oslo, Norway
Winner: Lena (Germany), 'Satellite'
UK entry: Josh Dubovie, 'That Sounds Good to Me' (25th)
Garry's Gold Medal: Jessy Matador (France), 'Allez Ola Olé'

Year: 2011
Location: Düsseldorf, Germany
Winner: Ell & Nikki (Azerbaijan), 'Running Scared'
UK entry: Blue, 'I Can' (11th)
Garry's Gold Medal: Poli Genova (Bulgaria), 'Na Inat'

Year: 2012
Location: Baku, Azerbaijan
Winner: Loreen (Sweden), 'Euphoria'
UK entry: Engelbert Humperdinck, 'Love Will Set You Free' (25th)
Garry's Gold Medal: Anmary (Latvia), 'Beautiful Song'

Year: 2013
Location: Malmö, Sweden
Winner: Emmelie de Forest (Denmark), 'Only Teardrops'
UK entry: Bonnie Tyler, 'Believe in Me' (19th)
Garry's Gold Medal: Anouk (the Netherlands), 'Birds'

Year: 2014
Location: Copenhagen, Denmark
Winner: Conchita Wurst (Austria), 'Rise Like a Phoenix'
UK entry: Molly, 'Children of the Universe' (17th)
Garry's Gold Medal: Emma (Italy), 'La Mia Città'

Year: 2015
Location: Vienna, Austria
Winner: Måns Zelmerlöw (Sweden), 'Heroes'
UK entry: Electro Velvet, 'I'm Still in Love with You' (24th)
Garry's Gold Medal: Sweden

Year: 2016
Location: Stockholm, Sweden
Winner: Jamala (Ukraine), '1944'
UK entry: Joe & Jake, 'You're Not Alone' (24th)
Garry's Gold Medal: Barei (Spain), 'Say Yay!'

Year: 2017
Location: Kiev, Ukraine
Winner: Salvador Sobral (Portugal), 'Amar Pelos Dois'
UK entry: Lucie Jones, 'Never Give Up on You' (15th)
Garry's Gold Medal: Ilinca feat. Alex Florea (Romania), 'Yodel It!'

Reprise: A Euphoric Selection

So who would I bring back to represent each country at the Eurovision Song Contest if I could meddle with the laws of time and space? I've restricted this list to (i) countries who competed in 2017 and (ii) countries not now competing but who've won the contest in the past (in the case of Yugoslavia, of course, the country now no longer exists). Where artists have appeared at Eurovision more than once, I've selected specific years. Reserves are in italics.

One more thing: I'd expect all of these to bring a new song with them. I don't want any re-treads.

Albania: Anjeza Shahini (2004) *Olta Boka (2008)*

Armenia: Iveta Mukuchyan (2016) *Inga & Anush (2009)*

Australia: Guy Sebastian (2015) *Dami Im (2016)*

Austria: Conchita Wurst (2014) *Springtime (1978)*

Azerbaijan: Dihaj (2017) *Elnur & Samir (2008)*

Belarus: Teo (2014) *Aleksandra & Konstantin (2004)*

Belgium: Telex (1980) *Fud Leclerc (1956)*

Bulgaria: Poli Genova (2016) *Deep Zone & Balthazar (2008)*

Croatia: Doris Dragović (1999) *Dragonfly ft. Dado Topić (2007)*

Cyprus: Minus One (2016) *Ivi Adamou (2012)*

Czech Republic: Gabriela Gunčiková (2016) *Tereza Kerndlová (2008)*

Denmark: Birthe Wilke (1959) *Kølig Kaj (1997)*

Estonia: Sandra Oxenryd (2006) *Malcolm Lincoln & Manpower 4 (2010)*

Finland: Lordi (2006) *Riki Sorsa (1981)*

FYR of Macedonia: Gjoko Taneski, Billy Zver & Pejčin (2010) *Martin Vucić (2005)*

France: Sebastien Tellier (2008) *Jessy Matador (2010)*

Georgia: Nina Sublatti (2015) *Eldrine (2011)*

Germany: Mekado (1994) *Dschinghis Khan (1979)*

Greece: Giorgos Alkaios & Friends (2010) *Helena Paparizou (2005)*

Hungary: Compact Disco (2012) *Friderika Bayer (1994)*

Iceland: Pollapönk (2014) *Silvia Night (2006)*

Ireland: Jedward (2011) *Linda Martin (1984)*

Israel: Dana International (1998) *Nadav Guedj (2015)*

Italy: Toto Cutugno (1990) *Francesco Gabbani (2017)*

Latvia: Brainstorm (2000) *Aminata (2015)*

Lithuania: LT United (2006) *InCulto (2010)*

Luxembourg: Anne-Marie David (1973) *France Gall (1965)*

Malta: Kurt Calleja (2012) *Morena (2008)*

Moldova: Zdob şi Zdub (2005) *SunStroke Project (2017)*

Monaco: Séverine (1971) *Séverine Ferrer (2006)*

Montenegro: Highway (2016) *Who See & Nina Žižić (2013)*

Netherlands: Frizzle Sizzle (1986) *Mouth & MacNeal (1973)*

Norway: Odd Børre (1968) *Bobbysocks! (1985)*

Poland: Blue Café (2004) *Ich Troje (2006)*

Portugal: Sofia Vitória (2004) *Da Vinci (1989)*

Romania: Ilinca feat. Alex Florea (2017) *Nicola (2003)*

Russia: Dima Bilan (2006) *Polina Gagarina (2015)*

San Marino: Serhat (2016) *Miodio (2008)*

Serbia: Milan Stanković (2010) *Sanja Vučić ZAA (2016)*

Slovenia: Tinkara Kovač (2014) *Maja Keuc (2011)*

Spain: Barei (2016) *Azúcar Moreno (1990)*

Sweden: ABBA (1974) *Tomas Ledin (1980)*

Switzerland: Vanilla Ninja (2005) *Lys Assia (1958)*

Turkey: Ajda Pekkan (1980) *Athena (2004)*

UK: Katrina & the Waves (1997) *Cliff Richard (1973)*

Ukraine: Svetlana Loboda (2009) *Verka Serduchka (2007)*

Yugoslavia: Baby Doll (1991) *Daniel (1983)*

Printed in Great Britain
by Amazon